Collector's Library

A Thousand and One Limericks

The limerick's callous and crude,
Its morals distressingly lewd;
    It's not worth the reading
    By persons of breeding –
It's designed for us vulgar and rude.

A Thousand and One
LIMERICKS

Editorial Selection by
**MARCUS CLAPHAM AND
ROSEMARY GRAY**

with an Introduction by
MARCUS CLAPHAM

Collector's Library

This edition first published 2009 by Collector's Library
an imprint of Pan Macmillan
20 New Wharf Road, London NI 9RR
Associated companies throughout the world
www.panmacmillan.com

ISBN 978-1-9057-1668-5

5

A CIP catalogue record for this book is available from the British Library.

Typeset by Antony Gray
Printed and bound in China by Imago

Contents

※

Introduction

While the limerick is a largely Anglo-American phenomenon, it is sometimes claimed that the first limerick was composed by Italian philosopher and theologian Thomas Aquinas (1225–1274):

> Sit vitiorum meorum evacuatio
> Concupiscentae et libidinis exterminatio,
> Caritatis et patientiae,
> Humilitatis et obedientiae,
> Omniumque virtutum augmentatio.
>
> (Let my viciousness be emptied,
> Desire and lust banished,
> Charity and patience,
> Humility and obedience,
> And all the virtues increased.)

It has the standard limerick rhyme-scheme of **a a b b a**, as do a number of later poems from Tom O'Bedlam and Shakespeare to James Boswell, but it is not until the nineteenth century that the limerick develops into the form that we know today. This was established by Edward Lear in his *Book of Nonsense*, published in 1846.

It should be noted that Lear did not call his

nonsense-verse 'limericks'. The origin of the term is, at best, a guess, and the commonest suggestion, in the *Oxford English Dictionary*, is that the name is 'from a custom at convivial parties, according to which each member sang an extemporised "nonsense-verse" which was followed by a chorus containing the words "Will you come up to Limerick".' Other than this, there is no Irish connection. The first instance of the use of 'limerick' to mean nonsense-verse the *OED* cites as being in 1896, and in *Stalky & Co* by Rudyard Kipling (1899) Stalky suggests that he and his companions should 'make up a good catchy limerick, and let the fags sing it'.

Edward Lear (1812–1888) was a remarkably fine artist, famed for his *Illustrations of the Family of the Psittacidae* (1832), but he was afflicted with ill health and gratefully accepted a post with Edward

Stanley, 13th Earl of Derby, who was a naturalist and an expert on parrots. Lear was a popular member of the household, especially with Derby's grandchildren, and it was for them that he composed his nonsense verses. For the most part, they are just that, and lack the punch-line of later limericks. They are frequently geographical, and in most of them the last word of the first line is repeated as the last word of the last line:

> There was an old man of Thermopylae,
>> Who never did anything properly;
>> But they said, 'If you choose
>> To boil eggs in your shoes,
>> You shall never remain in Thermopylae.'

Punch magazine published an unfunny limerick about Lord Brougham shortly before publication of *Nonsense Verse* but subsequently dropped the form (except for reviving it briefly in 1863 when *Nonsense Verse* was reprinted). However, the distinctive form turned up elsewhere in 1872, when a Cambridge undergraduate called A. C. Hilton contributed:

> There was a young gourmand of John's
> Who'd a notion of dining on swans;
>> To the Backs he took big nets
>> To capture the cygnets
> But was told they were kept for the Dons.

(It should be explained that St John's College, Cambridge which spans the River Cam is one of the few bodies entitled, under Royal licence, to cull and eat swans. A later and rather bawdier version is:

> There was a young student at John's
> Who wanted to bugger the swans,
> > But a loyal Head Porter
> > Said, 'Sir, take my daughter,
> Them swans is reserved for the Dons.')

By the late nineteenth century the form was beginning to acquire the characteristics that we know today. The rhyme scheme was established, as was the scansion, which was generally amphi-brachic (short, long, short – 'Whilst Titian was mixing rose madder') or anapaestic (two shorts and a long – 'From the depths of the crypt at St Giles'), and it became accepted practice that the final line should deliver an unexpected or decisive message to round off the verse.

In the Edwardian era of the early twentieth century, the popularity of the limerick was boosted by contests in newspapers and magazines which offered increasingly lavish prizes for completing a limerick, of which the first four lines were supplied by the competition setter. Winners might receive as much as £50 which was worth roughly £2,000 in today's money. After WWI, prizes were even more extravagant, and included a first prize of a freehold house, a horse and trap and £2 a week for life.

In the *Oxford Companion to the English Language*, Raymond Chapman pointed out that the limerick with its 'easy, swinging rhythm makes it particularly suitable for humorous or scurrilous verse, and for taboo subjects'. Publication in 1924 of Langford Reed's *The Complete Limerick Book*, with illustrations by H. M. Bateman, gave the form some respectabilty and it flourished. But the growth of ribald limericks is the chief characteristic of the period, and this aspect has given the form lasting appeal. Because of the often scurrilous content, it is assumed that most limerick authors are men – though since authorship of most limericks is anonymous it is difficult to prove – and it is fair to say that the limerick is not a preferred form for female writers. It is surprising that there seems to be no limerick attributed to Dorothy Parker, who would surely have embraced the genre gladly. Gershon Legman avers that one limerick that women seem to appreciate is:

'For the tenth time, dull Daphnis,' said Chloë,
'You have told me my bosom is snowy;
    You've made much verse on
    Each part of my person,
Now *do* something – there's a good boy.'

From the Contents page of this book it can be seen how varied are the subjects of limericks. From Edward Lear onwards, the prevalence of place-names is striking. 'There was a young man of . . . ' is so common an opening that it comes as a pleasant surprise to encounter 'Nymphomaniacal Jill', whose curiosity about high explosives led to such an unfortunate separation of her parts. Bishops of the great city of Birmingham are celebrated in many limericks, and their virility is affirmed five times in this anthology. With only an occasional example – The Bishop was 'nobody's fool/(He'd been to a great public school)' – it is perhaps surprising that there is no tradition of limericks relating to fee-paying schools. The same is not true of Oxford and Cambridge. St John's College, Cambridge has already been mentioned, the chaplain of King's College, Cambridge is cruelly mocked – and the incestuous 'Master of Jesus' must have been a Cambridge man because the head of Jesus College, Oxford is referred to as the Principal rather than the Master. The Warden and members of Wadham College, Oxford are accused three times of a particular sexual preference, while the pleasant north-Cornish resort of Bude shares with Wadham an inviting rhyme and is represented six times. The west-London suburbs of Ealing and Kew turn up five times, the county of Kent five, while Slough and Perth have four and Peru and Madrid have five and six entries respectively.

Though the limerick is subject to strict rules, they can be elegantly broken by what is known as 'the anti-limerick'. This form subverts the normal rules either by adding syllables or lines to the standard form, thus:

> There was a young man of Japan
> Who wrote verses that never would scan,
> When folk told him so
> He replied, 'Yes, I know,
> But I always try to get as many words into
> the last line as I can;'

or by deliberately flouting every rule, as with the famous Limerick by W. S. Gilbert:

> There was an old man of St Bees
> Who was stung on the arm by a wasp,
> When they asked, 'Does it hurt?'
> He replied, 'No, It doesn't,
> I thought all the time t'was a hornet!'

which is designed to confuse the reader with its ludic subversion of expectation. The 'young fellow named Skinner' similarly disconcerts in an un-canonical extra couplet.

The other main form of the anti-limerick plays

on words that are spelled one way but have an unusual pronunciation or are contractions of familiar words. One example is:

> There was a young curate of Salisbury
> Whose habits were halisbury-scalisbury;
>   He'd go biking in Hampshire
>   Without any pampshire
> Till the bishop insisted he walisbury –

where the reader has to know that the Latin abbreviation of the Roman name for Salisbury is 'Sarum' and that Hampshire is abbreviated to 'Hants', from its Latin root. Mark Twain wrote a limerick along these lines which is astonishingly accomplished considering its place in the early development of the limerick:

> A man hired by John Smith & Co.
> Loudly declared he would tho.
>   Man that he saw
>   Dumping dirt near his store,
> The drivers, therefore, didn't do.

'There was a young lady from Riga', one of the wittiest of all limericks, attributed to Cosmo Monk-house, was translated, equally wittily, into Latin:

> Puella Rigensis ridebat
> Quam tigris in tergo vehebat;
>   Externa profecta,

Interna revecta,
Sed risus cum tigre manebat;

and on the subject of translations, it would be a
pity to omit the mildly profane:

Il y avait un jeune homme de Dijon,
Qui n'avait que peu de religion,
Il dit, 'Quant à moi,
Je déteste tous les trois,
Le Père, et le Fils, et le Pigeon.'

Perhaps one other attribute of the limerick should
be mentioned, and that is the late development of
the internal rhyme. It seems that this occurs chiefly
in the ruder limericks and can be illustrated by:

There was a young girl from Baroda
Who built an erotic pagoda,
And the walls of its halls
Were festooned with the balls
And the tools of the fools that bestrode her.

Since Edward Lear's *Book of Nonsense* appeared
in 1846, contributions have been made to the
genre by many literary figures, including Mark
Twain, Robert Louis Stevenson, George Bernard
Shaw, Monsignor Ronald Knox, W. H. Auden,
Ogden Nash, Norman Douglas and Isaac Asimov.
There are other limerick anthologies, and inevit-
ably there is overlap between them. Langford Reed's

15

1924 collection has already been mentioned; it was full of printable rhymes. In 1928 Norman Douglas, perhaps jealous of D. H. Lawrence's success with *Lady Chatterley's Lover,* had privately printed in Portugal *Some Limericks: Collected for the use of Students, & ensplendour'd with Introduction, Geographical Index, and with Notes Explanatory and Critical*, a book of the bawdiest limericks that he could find, accompanied by a mock-critical apparatus. The commentary is very funny and most of the limericks surprisingly modern and very lewd. Louis Untermeyer and Bennett Cerf produced two of the best American anthologies of limericks, and their compatriot, Gershon Legman, has researched the limerick exhaustively and his writings on the subject are essential reading for the enthusiast. Perhaps the most enjoyable collection, inexplicably out of print, is W. S. Baring-Gould's *The Lure of the Limerick*, which combines a very fine selection with an immensely readable, scholarly account of the limerick's development.

Bibliography

Cerf, Bennett, *Out on a Limerick*, Harper, 1960

Douglas, Norman, *Some Limericks*, privately printed 1928; also Grove Press, 1967, and Anthony Blond, 1969

Legman, Gershon, *The Limerick: A History in Brief*, University Books Inc., 1964

Legman, Gershon, *The Limerick: 1,700 Examples, with Notes, Variants and Index*, Hautes Études, 1953

Marsh, Linda, *The Wordsworth Book of Limericks*, 1997

Reed, Langford, *The Complete Limerick Book*, Jarrold, 1924

Reed, Langford, *My Limerick Book*, Herbert Jenkins, 1937

Untermeyer, Louis, *Lots of Limericks: Light, Lusty and Lasting*, Garden City Press, 1961

Accidental,
Tragical
&
Regrettable

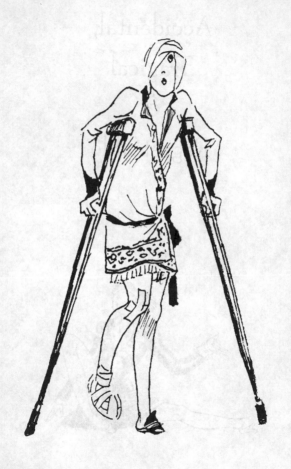

A certain young lady named Hannah
Was caught in a flood in Montana;
  As she floated away,
  Her beau, so they say,
Accompanied her on the piannah.

✳

Said a foolish householder of Wales,
'An odour of coal gas prevails.'
  She then struck a light
  And later that night
Was collected in seventeen pails.

✳

There was a young man of Cape Horn
Who wished he had never been born;
  And he wouldn't have been
  If his father had seen
That the end of the rubber was torn.

✳

There was an old man of Blackheath
Who sat on his set of false teeth.
  Said he with a start,
  'Oh Lor, bless my heart!
I have bitten myself underneath!'

✳

A short-sighted man from Havana
Confused clothing with flora and fauna;
   He was heard to say, 'Ouch,'
   When a black posing pouch
Turned out to be three small piranha.

✳

An unfortunate dumb mute from Kew
Was trying out signs that he knew;
   He did them so fast
   That his fingers at last
Got so tangled he fractured a few.

✳

Rebecca, a silly young wench,
Went out on the Thames to catch tench;
   When the boat was upset,
   She exclaimed, I regret,
A five-letter word – and in French!

✳

There was an old person of Ems
Who casually fell in the Thames;
   And when he was found,
   They said he was drowned,
That unlucky old person of Ems.

✳

There was an old lady of Rye,
Who was baked by mistake in a pie.
　　To the householder's disgust
　　She emerged in the crust
And exclaimed with a yawn, 'Where am I?'

✳

There was a young man who was bitten
By twenty-two cats and a kitten.
　　Cried he, 'It is clear
　　My end is quite near!
No matter, I'll die like a Briton.'

✳

A Tory, once out in his motor,
Ran over a Labourite voter.
　　'Thank goodness,' he cried,
　　'He was on the wrong side.
So I don't blame myself one iota.'

✳

A careless old cook of Saltash
With a second-hand car had a crash.
　　She ploughed through a wall,
　　House, garden and all,
And ended up banger and mash.

❋

There was an old man who when little
Fell casually into a kettle;
> But, growing too stout,
> He could never get out,
So he passed all his life in that kettle.

❋

There was a young fellow of Leeds
Who swallowed a packet of seeds.
> In a month, silly ass,
> He was covered in grass,
And he couldn't sit down for the weeds.

❋

There was an old fellow of Spain,
Whose leg was cut off by a train.
> When his friends said, 'How sad!'
> He replied, 'I am glad,
> For I've now lost my varicose veins.'

❋

There was a young lady of Glos.
Whose friends quite thought they had los.,
> When her handbag they spied
> Coming back from a ride
On the horns of a bull that had tos.

❋

There was a young fellow named Fisher
Who was fishing for fish in a fissure;
　　Then a cod with a grin
　　Pulled the fisherman in . . .
Now they're fishing the fissure for Fisher.

❋

There was a young lady named Psyche
Who was heard to ejaculate, 'Pcryche!'
　　For when riding her pbych,
　　She ran over a ptych,
And fell on some rails that were pspyche.

❋

An unskhylful rider from Rhyl
Motor-cycled full speed down a hyl,
　　Thyl a sphyl at a bend
　　Khyled our whylful young friend,
And he now in the churchyard lies sthyl.

❋

There was a young woman of Welwyn
Loved a barman, who served in the Belwyn.
　　But the Belwyn, oh dear!
　　Had a welwyn the rear,
So they never were wed, for they felwyn.

*

Said a man to his spouse in East Sydenham:
'My best trousers! Now where have you hydenham?
 It is perfectly true
 They were not very new,
But I foolishly left half a quydenham.'

*

It was hard on Apollo, I thought,
 When the workman who shifted him caught
  And broke off his penis,
  From malice or meanness,
And shipped him to England with naught.

*

A lass on the road to Goleen
 Met a baker with a drop of poteen;
  Five minutes of lovin'
  Put a bun in her oven,
The next time she won't be so keen.

*

There was an old maid of Duluth
 Who wept when she thought of her youth,
  And the glorious chances
  She'd missed at school dances;
And once in a telephone booth.

✳

A prudish old lady called Muir
Had a mind so incredibly pure
    That she fainted away
    At a friend's house one day
At the sight of a canary's manure.

✳

A prudish young girl of St Paul
Dreamt she'd undressed in the Mall.
    The best of the joke
    Was when she awoke,
And found mud on her backside and all.

✳

A girl who would not be disgraced,
Would flee from all lovers in haste.
    It all went quite well
    Till one day she fell . . .
She sometimes still dreams she is chaste.

✳

There was a young lady named Duff
With a lovely, luxuriant muff.
    In his haste to get in her,
    One eager beginner
Lost both of his balls in the rough.

✳

An Australian fellow named Menzies
By kissing sent girls into frenzies.
    But a virgin one night
    Crossed her legs in a fright
And shattered his bifocal lenses.

✳

Nymphomaniacal Jill
Tried a dynamite stick for a thrill.
    They found her vagina
    In North Carolina
And bits of her tits in Brazil.

✳

There was a young girl from Taipei
Who was voted the Queen of the May;
    But the pole she went round
    Wasn't stuck in the ground
But attached to a young man named Wei.

✳

There was a young girl of Pitlochry,
Who was had by a man in a rockery.
    She said: 'Oh! You've come
    All over my bum;
This isn't a fuck – it's a mockery.'

*

Young girls of seductive proportions
Should take contraceptive precautions.
  Silly young Ermyntrude
  Let one small sperm intrude . . .
Who's the best man for abortions?

*

There's a girl there on Marathon Key
Who gave my pal Flip the VD.
  Evil ways are a curse;
  Still, it might have been worse –
Had I called 'heads' it would have been me!

*

There was a young man of Bengal
Who went to a masquerade ball
  Arrayed like a tree,
  But he failed to foresee
His abuse by the dogs in the hall.

*

He hated to sew, so young Ned
Rang the bell of his neighbour instead;
  But her husband said, 'Vi,
  When you stitched his torn fly,
There was no need to bite off the thread.'

❋

A lady skin-diver, a Gemini,
Encountered a monstrous anemone
    Far under the sea.
    It seized her with glee,
And ate up her *pudenda feminae*.

❋

An impetuous couple named Kelly
Now go through life belly-to-belly:
    Because in their haste
    They used library paste
Instead of petroleum jelly.

❋

As the elevator car left our floor
Big Sue caught her teats in the door;
    She yelled a good deal,
    But had they been real,
She'd have yelled considerably more.

❋

There was a young sailor named Bates
Who danced the fandango on skates;
    He fell on his cutlass
    Which rendered him nutless
And practically useless on dates.

❋

When she danced at the Easter Parade,
Such a sexy impression she made
    That some lads from St Paul's,
    In tight jeans, hurt their balls
And had to be given first-aid.

❋

An accident really uncanny
Occurred to my elderly granny:
    She sat down in a chair
    While her false teeth lay there
And bit herself right in the fanny.

❋

A new servant-maid named Maria
Had trouble lighting the fire;
    The wood being green,
    She used gasoline . . .
Her position by now is much higher.

❋

A daring young lady of Guam
Observed, 'The Pacific's so calm
    I'll swim out for a lark.'
    She met a large shark,
'Let us now sing the Ninetieth Psalm.'

❋

A man in a bus queue at Stoke
Unzipped all his flies for a joke.
 An old man gave a shout
 And almost passed out
And a lady close by had a stroke.

❋

One Longbottom, climbing Ben Nevis,
Fell forty feet into a crevice.
 He was wedged by *ars longa*,
 Recovered, got stronger,
Then passed out – RIP, *vita brevis*.

❋

There was a young hiker called Hilda
Who went for a hike on St Kilda.
 They say that the climb
 Is really sublime:
But it wasn't for Hilda – it killed her.

❋

There was a young lady called Kitchener
Who slipped on the quayside at Itchenor.
  In spite of the pain,
  She laughed like a drain
While the surgeon inserted a stitch in her.

❋

A flatulent plumber called Hart
Could not get his blow lamp to start.
  So he then struck a match,
  Saying, 'Now it'll catch,'
Thus extinguishing Hart, lamp and fart.

❋

There was a young girl from Dundee
Who went down to the river to swim.
  A man in a punt
  Stuck an oar in her eye
And now she wears glasses, you see.

❋

There was a young fellow from Ongar
Who had to be barred from the congar.
  The heat of the dance
  Made his trousers advance,
As the congar got longar and longar.

✳

A housewife called out with a frown,
When surprised by some callers from town,
    'In a minute or less
    I'll slip on a dress.'
But she slipped on the stairs and came down.

✳

There was a young fellow named Hall
Who fell in the spring in the fall.
    'Twould have been a sad thing
    Had he died in the spring,
But he didn't, he died in the fall.

✳

A decrepit old gasman named Peter,
While hunting around his gas heater,
    Touched a leak with his light.
    He rose out of sight –
And, as everyone who knows anything about
poetry can tell you, he also ruined the meter.

✳

Evangeline Alice Du Bois
Committed a dreadful *faux pas*.
    She loosened a stay
    In her *décolleté*,
Exposing her *je ne sais quoi*.

35

❋

There was an old lady whose folly
Induced her to sit in a holly;
 Whereupon, by a thorn
 Her dress being torn,
She quickly became melancholy.

❋

An old couple living in Gloucester
Had a beautiful girl, but they loucester;
 She fell from a yacht,
 And never the spacht
Could be found where the cold waves
                        had toucester.

❋

There was a young fellow named Bliss
Whose sex life was sadly amiss,
 For even with Venus
 His recalcitrant penis
Would seldom do better than t
                              h
                              i
                              s.

Actual,
Factual
&
Paradoxical

There's a Portuguese person named Howell
Who lays on his lies with a trowel;
　　Should he give over lying,
　　'Twill be when he's dying,
For living is lying with Howell.

　As a beauty, I'm not a star,
　　There are many more handsome by far;
　　　But my face, I don't mind it,
　　　For I am behind it,
　It's the people in front get the jar.

There was a young lady of Kent
Who always said just what she meant.
　　People said, 'She's a dear –
　　So unique – so sincere – '
But they shunned her by common consent.

Concerning the bees and the flowers,
In the fields and the gardens and bowers;
　　You will tell at a glance
　　That their ways of romance
Haven't any resemblance to ours.

✳

In Paris some visitors go
To see what no person should know;
   And then there are tourists,
   The purest of purists,
Who say it is quite *comme il faut.*

✳

When Tommy first saw Colonel Peake
(Now, Tommy is five and can speak),
   He said, 'Auntie Rose,
   Does he put on his nose
The same stuff you paint on your cheek?'

✳

I sat next to the duchess at tea.
It was just as I feared it would be:
   Her rumblings abdominal
   Were simply phenomenal,
And everyone thought it was me!

✳

'What have I done?' said Christine:
'I've ruined the party machine.
   To lie in the nude
   Is not very rude,
But to lie in the House is obscene.'

✳

A youthful schoolmistress named Beauchamp
Said, 'These awful boys, how shall I teauchamp?
   For they will not behave
   Although I look grave
And with tears in my eyes I beseauchamp.

✳

A charming young lady named Geoghegan,
Whose Christian names are less peophegan,
   Will be Mrs Knollys
   Very soon at All Ksollys;
But the date is at present a veogheg 'un.

✳

A lady from way down in Ga.
Became quite a notable fa.
    But she faded from view
    With a quaint IOU
That she'd signed '(Miss) Lucrezia Ba'.

✳

A fellow who lived in New Guinea,
Was known as a silly young nuinea;
    He utterly lacked
    Good judgement and tacked
For he told a plump girl she was skuinea.

✳

The limerick's callous and crude,
Its morals distressingly lewd;
    It's not worth the reading
    By persons of breeding –
It's designed for us vulgar and rude.

✳

A finicky man from Australia
With the ladies was largely a failure.
    He said, 'Sex may be fun,
    But in the long run
It will damage my fine genitalia.'

❋

A young man from near Carrighart
Was known from Cork to Dundalk for his farts;
  When they asked: 'Why so loud?'
  He replied with head bowed:
'When I farts, sure I farts from the heart.'

❋

A woman from sweet Donegal
Who had triplets almost each fall
  Said, when asked how and wherefore,
  'Sure, that's what we're here for,
But oft-times we got nothing at all.'

❋

There was a young maiden from Multerry
Whose knowledge of life was desultory;
  She explained, like a sage:
  'Adolescence? The age
Between puberty and – er – adultery.'

❋

A luscious young maiden of Siam
Remarked to her lover, young Kayyam,
  'If you take me, of course,
  You must do it by force –
But, God knows, you're stronger than I am.'

43

✳

An observant young man of the West
Said, 'I've found out by personal test
   That men who make passes
   At girls who wear glasses
Have just as good fun as the rest.'

✳

Seducing shy virgins to sin
Takes more than sweet-talking and gin:
   An all-out seduction
   Is a major production –
It may take you days to get in.

✳

At the orgy I humped twenty-two,
And was glad when the whole thing was through;
   I don't find it swinging
   To do all this change-ringing,
But at orgies, what else can you do?

✳

A wanton young lady of Wimleigh,
Reproached for not acting more primly,
   Answered, 'Heavens above,
   I know sex isn't love,
But it's such an attractive facsimile!'

✳

There was a young girl named Priscilla
With whom sex proved quite simply a thriller.
   One just can't get enough
   Of that girl's kind of stuff,
Though the sixth time it's frankly a killer.

✳

   A comely young widow named Ransom
   Was ravished three times in a hansom.
      When she cried out for more,
      A voice from the floor
   Said, 'Madam, I'm Simpson, not Samson.'

❋

There was a young lady from Putney
Who was given to sexual gluttony;
    Warned a pious old duffer,
    'Your morals will suffer.'
'That's what you think,' she said. 'I ain't got any.'

❋

Have you heard of the boxer named Jules
Whose hunger for sex never cools?
    He pays no attention
    To social convention
Or the Marquis of Queensberry's rules.

❋

There was a young fellow in Maine
Who courted a girl all in vain;
    She cussed when he kissed her
    So he slept with her sister –
Again and *again* and again.

❋

'Last night,' said a lassie named Ruth,
'In a long-distance telephone booth,
    I enjoyed the perfection
    Of an ideal connection –
I was screwed, if you must know the truth.'

❋

Come to Noah's for wine and strong waters,
And for screwing in clean classy quarters.
    I assure every guest
    I've made personal test
Of my booze and my beds and my daughters.

❋

    Up the street sex is sold by the piece,
    And I wish that foul traffic would cease;
       It's a shame and improper,
       And I'd phone for a copper
    But that's where you'll find the police.

❋

A young girl was no good at tennis
But at swimming was really a 'menace';
    The cause, she explained,
    Was the way she had trained:
She had been a streetwalker in Venice.

❋

That luscious young harlot Miss Birks
(She's the pick of our local sex-works)
    Has serviced the mayor,
    A judge, the surveyor
And a newsboy (who normally jerks).

✳

'You know,' said the King of the Czechs,
'I too have a problem with sex;
  The men of my nation
  Prefer masturbation;
My women are physical wrecks.'

✳

There was a young man of St Paul's
Possessed the most useless of balls,
  Till at last, at the Strand,
  He managed a stand,
And tossed himself off in the stalls.

✳

'Active balls?' said an old man of Stoneham.
'I regret that I no longer own 'em.
  But I hasten to say
  They were good in their day –
De mortuis nil nisi bonum.'

✳

There was a young fellow of Warwick
Who had reason for feeling euphoric,
  For he could, by election,
  Have triune erection –
Ionic, Corinthian, Doric.

✳

Down in Berne, Minister Grew,
There's nothing that fellow won't screw –
    From queens down to cooks,
    They're all on his books,
And he dabbles in sodomy too.

✳

There was a young woman named Sally
Who loved an occasional dally –
    She sat on the lap
    Of a well-endowed chap
And said, 'Oo, you're right up my alley!'

❋

The pantyhose style is first-class
For revealing the shapely young lass;
   All the better to view her,
   But damn hard to screw her,
With those stockings up over her ass!

❋

'It's my custom,' said dear Lady Norris,
'To beg lifts from the drivers of lorries.
   When they get out to piss
   I see things that I miss
At the wheel of my two-seater Morris.'

❋

Some bird-watchers through their field-glasses
See flashes of heaving, bare arses.
   Now do you see why,
   Though bloodshot of eye,
Bird-watching appeals to the masses?

❋

What's reddish and roundish and hairy,
And hangs from a bush light and airy;
   Much hidden away
   From the broad light of day
Beneath a stiff prick? A gooseberry!

❋

There once was duchess named Sally
Who led her young page up an alley.
   She was quite out of luck,
   For the lad wouldn't fuck,
And she muttered, 'How green was my valet!'

❋

There was a young lady named Flo
Whose lover was almighty slow.
   So they tried it all night
   Till he got it just right,
For practice makes pregnant, you know.

❋

A naïve teenager, Miss Lewis,
Asked, 'What is it fellows do to us
    That makes babies come –
    Or am I just dumb?'
Her sister's reply was, 'They screw us.'

❋

A well-poised young lady named Sawyer
Claimed nothing could vex or annoy her.
    But the baby I fathered
    Had her all hot and bothered –
And I get nasty calls from her lawyer.

❋

There was a young lady of Maine
Who declared she'd a man on the brain.
    But you knew from the view
    Of her waist, as it grew,
It was not on her brain that he'd lain!

❋

There was a young girl of Cape Cod
Who thought babies were fashioned by God;
    But 'twas not the Almighty
    Who hiked up her nightie
But Roger the lodger – the sod!

✳

There was a young girl of Penzance
Who decided to take just one chance –
    She let herself go
    On the lap of her beau
And now all her sisters are aunts.

✳

There was a young lady of Wantage
Of whom the town clerk took advantage.
    Said the county surveyor,
    'Of course you must pay her;
You've altered the line of her frontage.'

✳

There was a young lady named Lynne
Who said, 'I'm prepared to begin
    Any sort of activity
    Which suits my proclivity,
Provided it counts as a sin.'

✳

There is a new Baron of Wokingham.
The girls say he don't care for poking 'em,
    Preferring 'Minette',
    Which is pleasant, but yet,
There is one disadvantage, he's choking 'em.

❋

There was a young lady called Hilda
Who went for a walk with a builder;
    He knew that he could,
    And he should and he would,
And he did, and it bloody near killed her.

❋

There was a young lady named White
Found herself in a terrible plight:
    A mucker named Tucker
    Had struck her, the fucker –
The bugger, the bastard, the shite!

❋

There was a young fellow called Clyde
Who once at a funeral was spied.
    When asked who was dead,
    He smilingly said:
'I don't know – I just came for the ride.'

❋

The limerick is furtive and mean:
You must keep it in close quarantine
    Or it sneaks to the slums
    And promptly becomes
Disorderly, drunk and obscene.

✳

In New Orleans dwelled a young Creole
Who, when asked if her hair was all reole,
    Replied with a shrug,
    'Just give it a tug
And decide by the way that I squeole.'

Said a Sassenach back in Dun Laoghaire,
'I pay homage to nationalist thaoghaire,
    But wherever I drobh
    I found signposts that strobh
To make touring in Ireland so draoghaire.'

✳

There was a young trollop from Trent
Who claimed not to know what they meant
    When men asked her age;
    She'd reply in a rage,
'My age is the age of consent.'

✳

There was a young lady of Louth
Who returned from a trip to the South.
    Her mother said: 'Nelly
    There's more in your belly
Than ever went in through your mouth.'

✳

Some gels – and I don't understand 'em –
Will strip off their clothing at random,
　　Without any qualms,
　　To exhibit their charms:
In short – *quod erat demonstrandum*.

✳

A canner, exceedingly canny,
One morning remarked to his granny:
　　'A canner can can
　　Anything that he can,
But a canner can't can a can, can he?'

✳

A colonial girl, sweet and sainted,
Was by war-striped young Indians tainted.
　　Later, asked of the ravages,
　　She said of the savages,
'They aren't as bad as they're painted.'

✳

The limerick packs laughs anatomical
Into space that is quite economical –
　　But the good ones I've seen
　　So seldom are clean,
And the clean ones so seldom are comical.

Anatomical,
Biological
&
Surreal

There was a young lady whose nose
Continually prospers and grows;
    When it grew out of sight,
    She exclaimed in a fright,
'Oh! Farewell to the end of my nose!'

✳

There was a young lady whose nose
Was so long that it reached to her toes;
    So she hired an old lady,
    Whose conduct was steady,
To carry that wonderful nose.

✳

There was a young lady whose eyes
Were unique as to colour and size;
    When she opened them wide,
    People all turned aside,
And started away in surprise.

✳

There was a young lady from Coleshill
Who incautiously sat on a mole's hill;
    An inquisitive mole
    Poked his nose up her hole –
The gal's OK but the mole's ill.

✳

There was a young maid who said, 'Why
Can't I look in my ear with my eye?
    If I give my mind to it,
    I'm sure I can do it –
You never can tell till you try.'

✳

There was an old lady of Kent,
Whose nose was remarkably bent.
    One day, they suppose,
    She followed her nose,
For no one knew which way she went.

✳

There was an old skinflint named Green
Who grew so abnormally lean
    And flat and compressed
    That his back squeezed his chest,
And sideways he couldn't be seen.

✳

An unfortunate lady named Piles
Had the ugliest bottom for miles;
    But her surgeon took pity
    And made it quite pretty:
All dimples, and poutings, and smiles.

❋

A singular fellow of Weston
Has near fifty feet of intestine;
   Though a signal success
   In the medical press,
It isn't much good for digestin'.

❋

There was a young lady named Grace
Who had eyes in a very odd place;
   She could sit on the hole
   Of a mouse or a mole
And stare the beast square in the face.

❋

There was a fat man from Lahore,
The same shape behind as before.
   They did not know where
   To offer a chair,
So he had to sit down on the floor.

❋

Cried a slender young lady named Toni,
With a bottom exceedingly bony,
   'I'll say this for my rump:
   Though it may not be plump,
It's my own, not a silicone phoney!'

✳

It is time to make love, douse the glim;
The evening sky becomes dim;
    The stars will soon peep
    As the birds fall asleep
And the loin shall lie down with the limb.

✳

There was a young girl named
Cholmondeley,
Witty, warm-hearted and colmondely.
    No girl could be finer,
    But she lacked a vagina –
A sad and arresting anolmondeley.

✳

The first time she saw a man nude,
Said a diffident lady named Wood:
    'I'm glad I'm the sex
    That's concave, not convex;
For I don't fancy things that protrude.'

✳

There were two young ladies of Grimsby,
Who said, 'What use can our quims be?
    We know that we piddle
    Through the hole in the middle
But what use can the hairs on the rims be?'

❋

A knight in a chapel in Ealing,
Who had spent several centuries kneeling,
   Said, 'Please keep off my arse
   When you're rubbing my brass:
It gives me a very strange feeling.'

❋

A naïve young lady of Bude
Had not seen a man in the nude;
   When a lewd fellow showed
   His all in the road,
She did not know what to conclude.

❋

On a blind date, the flirty Miss Rowe,
When asked for a fuck, answered, 'No!
   You can go second class
   (Shove your prick up my arse),
But I'm saving my cunt for my beau.'

❋

There was a young lady of Lynn
Who was nothing but bones except skin;
   So she wore a false bust
   In the likewise false trust
That she looked like a lady of sin

✳

There was a young lady named Mabel
Who liked to sprawl out on the table,
    Then cry to her man,
     'Stuff in all you can –
Your bollocks as well, if you're able.'

✳

There was a young fellow named Charteris
Put his hand where his young lady's garter is.
    Said she, 'I don't mind,
    And up higher you'll find
The place where my fucker and farter is.'

✳

The French are a race among races;
They fuck in the funniest places:
    Any orifice handy
    Is thought to be dandy,
Including the one in their faces.

✳

There was a young student named Jones
Who'd reduce any maiden to moans
    By his wonderful knowledge,
    Acquired in college,
Of nineteen erogenous zones.

✳

There was a young fellow named Meek
Who perfected a lingual technique;
   It drove women frantic
   But (much less romantic)
It chafed all the skin off his cheek.

✳

There was an old man of Connaught
Whose prick was remarkably short;
  When he got into bed,
  His old woman said,
'This isn't a prick, it's a wart.'

✳

There was once a newspaper vendor,
A person of dubious gender,
  Who'd agree, if you'd queue,
  To allow you to view
His remarkable double pudenda.

✳

There was a young lady of Fez
Who was known to the public as 'Jez'.
  Jezebel was her name,
  Sucking cocks was the game
She excelled at, so everyone says.

✳

'Of course,' said the Prince Palatine,
'I agree fornication is fine,
    But I entertain 'em
    Per os et per anum,
Which last I consider divine!'

✳

There was a young maiden named Rose
With erogenous zones in her toes.
    She remained onanistic
    Till a foot-fetishistic
Young man became one of her beaus.

✳

I know of a fortunate Hindu
Who is sought in the towns that he's been to
    By the ladies he knows,
    Who are thrilled to the toes
By the tricks he can make his foreskin do.

✳

There was a young lady of Norwood
Whose ways were provokingly forward.
    Her mother said, 'Dear,
    Please don't wriggle your rear
Like a trollop or tart or a whore would.'

❋

A modern young girl from Eau Claire
Remarked, as she sprawled in a chair,
   'I can tell from your glance
   I forgot to wear pants;
So stare at my crotch – I don't care!'

❋

To his bride said the lynx-eyed detective,
'Can it be that my eyesight's defective?
   Has your west tit the least bit
   The best of your east tit?
Or is it a trick of perspective?'

❋

There was a young fellow of Perth
Whose balls were the finest on earth;
   They grew to such size
   That one won a prize
And goodness knows what they were worth.

❋

There once was a Duchess of Bruges
Whose cunt was incredibly huge.
   Said the king to this dame
   As he thunderously came:
'Mon Dieu! Après moi, le déluge!'

✳

There was a young fellow named Hall
Who confessed, 'I have only one ball,
    But the size of my prick
    Is God's dirtiest trick
For the girls always ask, "Is that all?" '

✳

There was a young man from Berlin
Whose prick was the size of a pin.
    Said his girl, with a laugh,
    As she fondled his shaft,
'Well, this won't be much of a sin.'

✳

Pubic hair is put there for a reason
That is evident in the cold season:
    For the balls it's a muff,
    For the rod it's a ruff;
And it keeps the vagina from freezin'.

✳

There was a young man of Devizes
Whose balls were of different sizes.
    One was so small
    It was no ball at all
But the other was large, and won prizes.

✳

There was a young man of Nantucket
Whose prick was so long he could suck it:
   He said with a grin
   As he wiped off his chin,
'If my ear were a cunt I could fuck it.'

✳

A well-equipped fellow in school
Has the whole class admiring his tool.
   This magnificent dong
   Is quite twelve inches long,
Though it isn't much use as a rule.

✳

There once was a handsome young sheik
With a marvellous penile physique.
   Its length and its weight
   Made it look really great,
But he fell very short on technique.

✳

There was a young man of Ghent
Whose tool was so long that it bent;
   To save himself trouble,
   He put it in double,
And instead of coming, he went.

❋

There was a young lady of Twickenham
Who thought men had not enough prick in 'em.
  On her knees every day
  To God she would pray
To lengthen and strengthen and thicken 'em.

❋

There was a young lady named Brent
With a cunt of enormous extent,
  And so deep and so wide,
  The acoustics inside
Were so good you could hear when you spent.

❋

There was a young man of Coblenz
The size of whose balls was immense.
  One day, playing soccer,
  He sprang his left knocker,
And kicked it right over the fence.

❋

A vigorous fellow named Bert
Was attracted by every new skirt –
  Oh, it wasn't their minds
  But their rounded behinds
That excited this lovable flirt.

✱

There was a young lady of Bude
Who walked down the street in the nude.
   A policeman said, 'Whatumm
   Magnificent bottom!'
And slapped it as hard as he could.

✱

Said a chic and attractive young Greek,
'Would you like a quick peek that's unique?'
   'Why, yes,' Joe confessed,
   So she quickly undressed
And showed him her sleek Greek physique.

✱

There was a young lady called Etta
Who fancied herself in a sweater;
   Three reasons she had:
   Keeping warm was not bad,
But the other two reasons were better.

✱

Her husband is in the Hussars,
A colonel, all covered with scars;
   But it isn't his weals
   For which nightly she feels,
But the privates he lost in the wars.

❋

A young woman from old Montreal
Reminisced once concerning her fall,
    Saying, 'He was so quick,
    And his prick was so slick,
That I just never felt it at all!'

❋

There was a young lady of Perth
Who said, 'Lord! I'm increasing in girth!'
    And her lovely young figure
    Grew steadily bigger
And bigger – till after the birth.

❋

After lunch the Grand Duchess of Teck
Announced, 'If you'll listen one sec,
    We've found a man's tool
    In the small swimming pool,
So would all of you gentlemen check?'

❋

There was a young man of Bengal
Who swore he had only one ball,
    But two little bitches
    Unbuttoned his britches,
And found he had no balls at all.

❋

There was a young sailor from Brighton
Who remarked to his girl, 'You're a tight one.'
   She replied, ' 'Pon my soul,
   You're in the wrong hole;
There's plenty of room in the right one.'

❋

   A buxom young lady of Bude
   Remarked: 'Men are exceedingly rude –
      When I bathe in the sea
      They all follow me
   To see if my bosoms protrude.'

❋

At shooting, Miss Myra MacLeod
With exceptional gifts was endowed.
   But it wasn't her pistols
   So much as her bristols
That Myra's admirers admired.

❋

There was a young fellow called Jones
Whose fiancée had prominent bones
   And more than her share
   Of superfluous hair
Around her erogenous zones.

✳

There was a young eunuch from Tonga
Who made up a dance called the Conga.
  After dancing all day
  He heard his Queen say,
'I do wish your conga were longer.'

✳

There were once two young people of taste
Who were beautiful down to the waist.
  So they limited love
  To the region above
And thus remained perfectly chaste.

✳

There was a young girl from Bayeux
Whose hemlines got hayeux and hayeux.
  But the size of her thighs
  Provoked only surprise
And extinguished the flames of desayeux.

✳

A bobby from Effingham Junction,
Whose organ had long ceased to function,
  Deceived his good wife,
  For the rest of her life
With the aid of his constable's truncheon.

Anecdotal,

Circumstantial

&

Opportunistical

There was once a young man of Oporto
Who daily got shorter and shorter;
   The reason he said
   Was the hod on his head,
Which was filled with the heaviest mortar.

✳

A newspaper writer named Fling
Could make copy from most anything;
   But the copy he wrote
   Of a ten-dollar note
Was so good he is now in Sing Sing.

✳

There was a young man so benighted,
He never knew when he was slighted.
   He went to a party,
   And ate just as hearty
As if he'd been really invited.

✳

On an outing with seventeen Czechs,
A girl tourist supplied the free sex.
   She returned from the jaunt
   Feeling more or less gaunt,
But the Czechs were all absolute wrecks.

77

❋

A visitor once to Loch Ness
Met the monster, who left him a mess;
    They returned his entrails
    By the regular mails
And the rest of the stuff by express.

❋

There was a young person from Perth
Who was born on the day of his birth.
    He was married, they say,
    On his wife's wedding day,
And died when he quitted this earth.

❋

There was a brave damsel of Brighton
Whom nothing could possibly frighten.
    She plunged in the sea
    And, with infinite glee,
Sailed away on the back of a triton.

❋

There was a young girl of West Ham
Who hastily jumped on a tram.
    When she had embarked
    The conductor remarked,
'Your fare, miss.' She answered, 'I am.'

*

A society climber from Crewe
Enquired, 'What on earth shall I do?
   I of course know what's what,
   But I fear I have not
The faintest idea of who's who.'

*

There was a great lord in Japan
Whose name on a Tuesday began;
   It carried through Sunday
   Till twilight on Monday,
And sounded like stones in a can.

*

A publisher went off to France,
In search of a tale of romance;
   A Parisian lady
   Told a story so shady
That the publisher made an advance.

*

There was an old justice, named Percival,
Who said, 'I suppose you'll get worse if I'll
   Send you to gaol,
   So I'll put you on bail.'
Now wasn't Judge Percival merciful?

✳

There was a sweet girl of Decatur
Who went to sea on a freighter.
    She was screwed by the master –
    An utter disaster –
But the crew all made up for it later.

✳

All was well with the dowager duchess
When trapped in a mad rapist's clutches,
    Till he turned on the light,
    Took one look, said good-night –
So she hit him with one of her crutches.

✳

There was a fat lady of Clyde
Whose shoelaces once came untied;
    She feared that to bend
    Would display her rear end,
So she cried and she cried and she cried.

✳

There was an old fellow of Tyre
Who constantly sat on the fire.
    When asked, 'Are you hot?'
    He said, 'Certainly not –
I'm James Winterbottom, Esquire.'

✻

A certain young laddie named Robbie
Rode his steed back and forth in the lobby;
   When they told him, 'Indoors
   Is no place for a horse,'
He replied, 'Well, you see, it's my hobby.'

✻

Said the Duke to the Duchess of Avery,
'Forgive me for breaking your reverie;
   You've been sitting on *Punch*
   Since long before lunch –
Might I have it, before it's unsavoury?'

✳

There was a young lady of Zion
Looked round for a shoulder to cry on;
   So she married a spouse
   From a very old house
And started to cry on the scion.

✳

A horrible brat from Belgravia
Drove his parents to thoughts of Our Savia.
   'By Jesus,' they swore,
   'We can't stand much more
Of this sonofabitch's behavia!'

✳

A Scots sailor, name of McPhie,
Who spoonerised to a degree,
   Once shouted, 'A wanker!'
   Instead of, 'Weight anchor!'
And spoke of himself as 'PhcMie'.

✳

A bather whose clothing was strewed
By breezes that left her quite nude,
   Saw a man come along
   And, unless I am wrong,
You expected this line to be rude.

✳

The fabulous Wizard of Oz
Retired from the business, becoz
   What with up-to-date science,
   To most of his clients
He wasn't the wizard he woz.

✳

A sensitive lady from Worcester
At a ball met a fellow who gorcester;
   A lecherous guy
   With blood in his uy,
So she ducked out before he sedorcester.

✳

Once out on the lake at Dubuque,
A girl took a sail with a duque;
   He remarked, 'I am sure
   You are honest and pure' –
And then leaned far over to puque.

✳

There was a mechalnwick of Alnwick
Whose opinions were anti-Germalnwick.
   So when war had begun
   He went off with a gun
The proportions of which were Titalnwick.

❈

A young man of Gloucester, named Foucester,
Had a wife who ran off with a coucester.
    He traced her to Leicester
    And tried to arreicester,
But in spite of these efforts he loucester.

❈

There was a young lady named Wemyss
Who it semyss was troubled with dremyss;
    She would wake in the night
    And in terrible fright
Shake the bemyss of her house with her scremyss.

❈

A young Irish servant in Drogheda
Had a mistress who often annogheda,
    Whereon she would swear
    With language so rare
That thereafter nobody emplogheda.

❈

Said a lively young nursemaid in Padua
To her master, 'Please, sir, you're a dadua.
    I've come for some pins
    For to wrap up the quins
And to hear you remark, sir, how gladua.'

❋

Said the Duchess of Alba to Goya:
'Paint some pictures to hang in my foya!'
    So he painted her twice:
    In the nude, to look nice,
And then in her clothes, to annoya.

❋

Whilst Titian was mixing rose madder,
His model posed nude on a ladder.
    Her position to Titian
    Suggested coition
So he climbed up the ladder and had her.

*

There once was a sculptor named Phidias
Who had a distaste for the hideous;
   So he sculpt Aphrodite
   Without any nightie,
Which shocked the ultra-fastidious.

*

There was an old man of Nantucket
Who kept all his cash in a bucket.
   His daughter, called Nan,
   Ran away with a man,
And as for the bucket, Nantucket.

*

Pa followed the pair to Pawtucket
(The man and the girl with the bucket),
   And he said to the man,
   'You're welcome to Nan!'
But as for the bucket, Pawtucket.

*

Then the pair followed Pa to Manhasset,
Where he still held the cash as an asset;
   And Nan and the man
   Stole the money and ran,
And as for the bucket, Manhasset.

*

There was a blackguard from near Croom,
Who lured a poor girl to her doom.
    He not only seduced her,
    But robbed her and goosed her
And left her to pay for the room.

*

There was an old maid of Pitlochry
Whose morals were truly a mockery,
    For under the bed
    Was a lover instead
Of the usual porcelain crockery.

*

There was a young lady of Pecking
Who indulged in a great deal of necking;
    This seemed a great waste
    Since she claimed to be chaste;
This statement, however, needs checking.

*

An erstwhile old maid of Vancouver
Caught her man by an artful manoeuvre;
    For she jumped on his knee
    As he dozed by the sea;
Now, nothing on earth can remove her.

✳

A spinster who came from the Ruhr
Was grasped by a vulgar young boor.
   This detestable varmint
   Unfastened her garment,
But proved to be just a voyeur.

✳

When he raped an old maid on the train,
They arrested a fellow named Braine.
   But the ex-virgin cried,
   'That's for me to decide,
And I'd be the last to complain!'

✳

What he asked for (a four-letter word),
Badly frightened the virgin Miss Byrd;
   But gin and insistence
   Wore down her resistance.
The four-letter word then occurred.

✳

Two middle-aged ladies from Fordham
Went out for a walk, and it bored 'em.
   As they made their way back,
   A sex maniac
Leapt out from the woods, and ignored 'em.

❋

A woman who lived near Cape Fear
Would always most carefully steer
   Past men whom she saw,
   But was brought to the floor
By a well-timed attack from the rear.

❋

An amorous maiden antique
Locked a man in her house for a week;
   He entered her door
   With a shout and a roar
But his exit was marked by a squeak.

❋

A homely old spinster of France,
Whom all the men looked at askance,
   Threw her skirt over head
   And then jumped into bed
Saying, 'Now I've at least half a chance.'

❋

A rapist, who reeked of cheap booze,
Attempted to ravish Miss Hughes;
   She cried: 'I suppose
   There's no time for my clothes,
But please let me take off my shoes!'

*

A young lady sat on a quay,
Just as proper as proper could be,
  A young fellow goosed her
  And roughly seduced her,
So she thanked him and went home to tea.

*

Of her 'opening night' near Fort Bliss
She explained, 'It began with a kiss,
  And ended in bed
  With a torn maidenhead
And my eyeballs both rolling like this!'

*

On Matilda's white bosom there leaned
The cheek of a low-minded fiend,
  But she yanked up his head
  And sarcastically said,
'My boy! Won't you ever be weaned?'

*

There is a young woman from Riga
With morals depressingly meagre,
  She's seduced twice a week
  By a lecherous Greek –
If 'seduced' is the word when she's eager.

❊

There was a young maid of Ostend,
Who swore she'd hold out to the end;
   But alas, half way over,
    'Twixt Calais and Dover,
She'd done what she didn't intend.

❊

There was a young person named May,
Who never let men have their way;
   But one brawny young spark
    One night in the park . . .
Now she goes to the park every day.

✲

An uptight young lady named Brearley,
Who valued her morals too dearly,
    Had sex, so I hear,
    Only once every year,
Which strained her pudenda severely.

✲

A candid young girl named McMillan
Replied to an arrogant villain
    Who leered, 'Now I'll rape you!'
    'I cannot escape you;
But rape me you'll not, for I'm willin'.'

✲

There was a young maid of Peru,
Who swore she never would screw –
    Except under stress
    Or forceful duress,
Like: 'I'm ready. How about you?'

✲

A lisping young lady called Beth
Was saved from a fate worse than death
    Seven times in a row,
    Which unsettled her so
That she stopped saying 'No' and said 'Yeth'.

✳

There was a young writer named Smith,
Whose virtue was largely a myth;
   We knew that he did it –
   He couldn't have hid it –
The question was only who with.

✳

There was a young girl called Bianca,
Who slept while her ship lay at anchor;
   She awoke with dismay
   When she heard the mate say:
'Hi! Hoist up the top sheet and spanker!'

✳

There's a very prim girl called McDrood;
What a combo – both nympho and prude!
   She wears her dark glasses
   When fellows make passes,
And keeps her eyes shut when she's screwed.

✳

A lovely young girl named Ann Heuser
Declared that no man could surprise her,
   But a fellow named Gibbons
   Untied her Blue Ribbons
And now she is sadder Budweiser

*

There was a young lady called Kate
Who necked in the dark with her date;
  When asked how she fared,
  She said she was scared
But otherwise doing first-rate.

*

There was a young lady of Florence
Who for kissing professed great abhorrence;
  But when she'd been kissed,
  And found what she'd missed,
She wept till her tears came in torrents.

*

There's a pretty young lady named Sark,
Afraid to get laid in the dark,
  But she's often manhandled
  By the light of a candle
In the bushes of Gramercy Park.

*

Said a voice from the back of the car,
'Young man, I don't know who you are,
  But allow me to state,
  Though it may come too late,
I had not meant to go quite this far.'

✻

There was a young lady named Hunt
Who performed the unusual stunt
 Of screwing by mail
 When she was in jail,
For she had a delectable cunt.

✻

There was a young fellow called Lancelot,
Whom his neighbours all looked on
        askance a lot:
 Whenever he'd pass
 A presentable lass,
The front of his pants would advance a lot.

✻

There was a young lady called Maud,
A sort of society fraud;
 In the parlour, 'tis told,
 She was distant and cold,
But on the verandah, my Gawd!

✻

There was a young wife from Peoria
 Who checked into the Waldorf-Astoria,
  Where she stayed for a week
  With two Swedes and a Greek
In a state of near-total euphoria.

❋

There was a young lady of Lynn
Who was deep in original sin;
　　When they said, 'Do be good!'
　　She said, 'Would if I could!'
And straightway went at it again.

❋

A certain hard-working young hooker
Was such an enchanting good-looker
　　There were fights 'mongst the fuzz
　　Over whose turn it was
To pinch her, and frisk her, and book her.

❋

There was a mechalnwick of Alnwick
Whose opinions were anti-Germalnwick.
　So when war had begun
　He went off with a gun
The proportions of which were Titalnwick.

❋

There was a young girl of Darjeeling,
Who danced with such exquisite feeling;
　　There was never a sound
　　For miles around,
Save of fly-buttons hitting the ceiling.

✱

A plumber from Lowater Creek
Was called in by a dame with a leak.
  She looked so becoming
  He fixed all her plumbing
And didn't emerge for a week.

✱

There once was a dentist named Stone
Who saw all his patients alone.
  In a fit of depravity
  He filled the wrong cavity,
And my! how his practice has grown!

✳

There was a young girl of St Cyr,
Whose reflex reactions were queer;
   Her escort said: 'Mabel!
   Get up off the table!
That money is there for the beer.'

✳

There was a young man of high station
Who was found by a pious relation
   Making love in a ditch
   To – I won't say a bitch –
But a woman of no reputation.

✳

There was a young girl from Baroda
Who built an erotic pagoda.
   The walls of its halls
   Were festooned with the balls
And the tools of the fools who bestrode her.

✳

An uncertain young woman named Fern
Was so great she had lovers to burn;
   She got into bed
   With both Johnnie and Fred
And didn't know which way to turn.

✳

There was a young woman named Susan
Who found it completely amusing
　　To make love to three men –
　　Although who did what when
Was frequently rather confusing.

✳

There was a young lady of Glamis
Who'd undress without any qualms.
　　She would strip to the buff
　　For enough folding stuff
And freely dispose of her charms.

✳

There was a young lady named Brooke
Who never could learn how to cook.
　　But on a divan
　　She could please any man –
She knew every damn trick in the book!

✳

A young ghost from old Bangladesh
Went out with a girl and got fresh.
　　She said, 'I don't mind
　　High spirits, you'll find,
But I won't have you come in the flesh.'

✳

A forward young fellow named Tarr
Had a habit of goosing his ma;
   'Go pester your sister,'
   She said, when he kissed her,
'I've trouble enough with your pa.'

✳

There was an old man from Fort Drum
Whose son was incredibly dumb;
   When he urged him ahead
   He went down instead,
For he thought to succeed meant succumb.

✳

There was a young lady of Condover
Whose husband had ceased to be fond of her.
   He could not forget
   He had wooed a brunette
But peroxide had now made a blonde of her.

✳

Poor old Robinson Crusoe!
He had no woman to screw, so
   He'd sit on a rock
   And play with his cock
(Or he'd get his man Friday to do so).

✳

Said another young woman of Croft,
Amusing herself in the loft,
  'A salami or wurst
  Is what I should choose first –
With bologna you know you've been boffed.'

✳

There was a young girl named Miss Randall
Who thought it beneath her to handle
  A young fellow's pole,
  So, instead, her hot hole
She contented by means of a candle.

✳

A man hired by John Smith & Co.
Loudly declared he would tho.
  Man that he saw
  Dumping dirt near his store.
The drivers, therefore, didn't do.

✳

There was a young woman called Maud
Who found herself now and then floored –
  Or bedded, or chaired,
  Or top-of-the-staired –
Oh, well, it's the life of a bawd.

✳

There was a young lady named Eva
Who went to a ball as Godiva,
   But a change in the lights
   Showed a tear in her tights,
And a low fellow present yelled, 'Beaver!'

✳

There was a young girl from Australia
Who dressed for a ball as a dahlia;
   When the petals uncurled
   They revealed to the world
That the dress as a dress was a failure.

✳

A daring young maid from Dubuque
Risked a rather decided rebuke
   By receiving a prude
   In the absolute nude,
But he gasped, 'If you only could cook!'

✳

There once was a young man named Murray
Who made love to his girl in a surrey.
   She started to sigh
   But someone came by
So he fastened his pants in a hurry.

✻

When the Bermondsey bricklayers struck,
Bill Bloggins was 'aving a fuck,
  By union rules
  He 'ad to down tools –
Now wasn't that bloody 'ard luck!

✻

A free-loving damsel named Hall
Once went to a birth-control ball.
  She took an appliance
  To make love with science
But nobody asked her at all.

✻

There was a young man of Penzance
Who rogered his three maiden aunts.
  Though them he defiled,
  He never got them with child,
Through using the letters of France.

✻

There was a young man of Belgravia,
Who cared neither for God nor his Saviour.
  He walked down the Strand
  With his balls in his hand,
And was had up for indecent behaviour.

❋

There was a young man of Hong Kong
Who invented a topical song.
   It wasn't the words
   That bothered the birds
But the horrible double ontong.

❋

I dined with the Duchess of Lee,
Who asked: 'Do you fart when you pee?'
   I said with some wit:
   'Do you belch when you shit?'
And felt it was one up to me.

❋

There was a young man from Kilbride
Who fell down a sewer and died.
   Now he had a brother
   Who fell down another;
And now they're interred side by side.

❋

A railway official at Crewe
Met an engine one day that he knew;
   Though he smiled and he bowed,
   That engine was proud:
It cut him – it cut him in two!

There was a young fellow from Tyne
Put his head on the South-Eastern Line;
   But he died of *ennui*,
   For the five fifty-three
Didn't come till a quarter past nine.

There was an old man who averred
He had learned how to fly like a bird;
   Cheered by thousands of people,
   He leapt from the steeple –
This tomb states the date it occurred.

✻

There was a young girl of Tralee,
Whose knowledge of French was, 'Oui, oui.'
   When they said: 'Parlez-vous?'
   She replied: 'Same to you!'
And was famed for her bright repartee.

✻

There was a young lady of Twickenham
Whose shoes were too tight to walk quickenham;
   She came back from a walk
   Looking whiter than chalk
And took them both off and was sickenham.

✻

There was a young Spaniard from Sitges
Who kept all the tourists in stitges
   By parading around
   With an ominous frown
And a banana in front of his britges.

✻

She frowned and called him Mr.
Because he boldly kr.,
   And so in spite
   That very night
This Mr. Kr. Sr.

✳

For years all the young men had struthven
To seduce a young lady called Ruthven;
    Once a plumber called Bert
    Got his hand up her skirt
And his plumbing was never forguthven.

✳

A colonel called out with great force
In the midst of Hyde Park for a horse.
    All the soldiers looked round
    But none could be found:
So he just rhododendron. Of course.

✳

A depraved young Parsee in Calcutta
Tried to write a rude word on a shutter.
    He had got to CU
    When a pious Hindu
Knocked him A over T in the gutter.

✳

There was a prim maiden called Campbell
Who got tangled one day in a bramble.
    She cried, 'Ouch, how it sticks –
    But so many great pricks
Are not met every day on a ramble.'

✳

There was a young lady from Reading
Who thought only plants were for bedding.
   But she took to the pill
   And went swiftly downhill –
And nobody danced at her wedding.

✳

There was a dumb lady from York
Who at flesh-to-flesh contact would balk.
   'Don't you think that you are
   [Said she] going too far?
Why can't we just sit here and talk?'

✳

There was young lady named Choate,
Whose pleasure it was to emote.
   She would say with a tear,
   'I am not wanted here!'
Then get up and take off her coat.

✳

A bottle of perfume that Willie sent
Was highly displeasing to Millicent.
   Her thanks were so cold
   That they quarrelled, I'm told,
Through that silly scent Willie sent Millicent.

Clerical, Spiritual
&
Theological

God's plan made a hopeful beginning,
But Man spoilt his chances by sinning;
  We trust that the story
  Will end in great glory,
But at present, the other side's winning.

✷

Said a wicked old madam named Belle,
Whom the preacher was threatening with Hell,
  'I have no regrets,
  No doubts – and no debts,
If I haven't done good, I've done well.'

✷

There was an old Fellow of Trinity,
A doctor well versed in Divinity,
  But he took to free thinking,
  And then to deep drinking,
And so had to leave the vicinity.

✷

A responsive young girl from the East
In bed was an able artiste.
  She had learned two positions
  From family physicians,
And ten more from the old parish priest.

✳

There was a young parson, called Perkins,
Exceedingly fond of small gherkins.
    One summer at tea
    He ate forty-three,
Which pickled his internal workins.

✳

Our vicar is good Mr Inge,
One evening he offered to sing,
    So we asked him to stoop,
    Put his head in a loop,
And pulled at each end of the string.

✳

The Bishop of Ibu Plantation
Wrote a thesis on transfiguration
    For the *Christian Review*
    (As all good bishops do)
While practising miscegenation.

✳

There once was a pious young priest
Who lived almost wholly on yeast.
    'For,' he said, 'it is plain
    We must all rise again,
And I want to get started, at least.'

✳

There was a young priest of Dun Laoghaire
Who stood on his head in the *Kyrie*;
   When people asked why,
   He said in reply:
'It's the latest liturgical theory.'

✳

A minister up in Vermont
Keeps a goldfish alive in the font;
   When he dips the babes in
   It tickles their skin,
Which is all that the innocents want.

✳

There was a young friar named Borrow
Who eloped with two nuns, to his sorrow.
   They lived on an isthmus,
   And one he named Christmas,
The other he christened Tomorrow.

✳

There was a young lady of Cheadle
Who sat down in church on a needle;
   Though deeply embedded,
   'Twas luckily threaded,
So she had it removed by the beadle.

❋

An old Quaker person of Fratton
Would sit in the church with his hat on.
  'When I wake up,' he said,
  'With my hat on my head,
I'm sure that it hasn't been sat on.'

❋

A clergyman told from his text
How Samson was scissored and vexed;
  Then a barber arose
  From his sweet Sunday doze,
Got rattled and shouted, 'Who's next?'

❋

There was a young curate of Salisbury
Whose habits were halisbury-scalisbury;
  He'd go hiking in Hampshire
  Without any pampshire
Till the bishop insisted he walisbury.

❋

There once was a boring young rev.
Who preached till it seemed he would nev.
  His hearers, *en masse*,
  Got a pain in the ass
And prayed for relief of their neth.

*

At Harvard, a randy old dean
Said: 'The funniest jokes are obscene.
   To bowdlerise wit
   Takes the shit out of it –
Who wants a limerick clean?'

*

A priest who got up with the dawn,
Saw a lass near a bush in Gougane:
   'Excuse me, dear miss,
   It's sinful to piss
On the sacred and blessed green lawn.'

*

There was a young lady near Glin
Who was strong on Original Sin.
   The priest said: 'Do be good.'
   She said: 'I would if I could,'
And started all over again.

*

There was a young lassie from Crosser,
Who in spiritual things was a messer.
   When sent to the priest,
   This lewd little beast,
Did her best to seduce her confessor

✳

I'm saying me prayers to St Jude
To keep away thoughts that are lewd.
   He'll do what he can
   To get me a man
And we'll wed, and we'll bed, is that rude?

✳

A clergyman's bride, very chaste,
Who wanted a child in great haste,
   Said, 'Mother, I grieve
   I shall never conceive:
I just cannot get used to the taste.'

✳

There was a young harlot from Leigh
Who slipped into church for a pee.
   Without any malice
   She pissed in the chalice
While singing the *Agnus Dei*.

✳

There was an old harlot from Dijon
Who in her old age got religion.
   'When I'm dead and gone,'
   Said she, 'I'll take on
The Father, the Son and the Pigeon.'

✳

A deacon, unhappily wed,
Thought to screw a black pig in his bed.
  Now the prick of the pig
  's undeniably big,
And it cork-screwed the deacon instead.

✳

There never was anything neater
Than the Bishop of Rochester's peter.
  In the heat of a clinch
  It would swell from an inch
To just a bit short of a metre.

✳

The tool of the Bishop of Truro
Was a rich colorado maduro,
   Said a real *cognoscenta*,
   'His balls were magenta,
Shot through with chiaroscuro.'

✳

When the Bishop of Solomon's diocese
Was stricken with elephantiasis,
   The public beheld
   His balls as they swelled
By paying exorbitant priocese.

✳

Said a priest to a quite famous beauty,
'I think that it's my bounden duty
   To give you the measure
   Of my tip for your pleasure –
And by "tip" I don't mean a gratuity.'

✳

There was an old prelate of Fife
Who had left, in the course of his life,
   Scores of well-rounded ends
   Of the wives of his friends
And likewise the friends of his wife.

❋

There was a young lady of Tottenham,
Her manners – she'd completely forgotten 'em;
    While at tea at the vicar's,
    She took off her knickers,
Explaining she felt much too hot in 'em.

❋

A handsome young monk in a wood
Told a girl she should cling to the good.
    She obeyed him, but gladly,
    He repulsed her, but sadly,
And said she had misunderstood.

❋

There was a young monk from Siberia
Whose morals were very inferior;
    He did to a nun
    What he shouldn't have done,
And now she's a Mother Superior.

❋

There were two young ladies of Birmingham
And this is the story concerning 'em:
    They lifted the frock
    And tickled the cock
Of the bishop as he was confirming 'em.

✳

The bishop was nobody's fool
(He'd been to a great public school);
    He took down their frillies
    And dealt with those fillies
With his twelve-inch episcopal tool.

✳

But that didn't bother the two:
They said, as the bishop withdrew,
    'The vicar is quicker
    And thicker and slicker
And longer and stronger than you.'

✳

Said the bishop, 'Of course, you are right.
The vicar's a man of great might;
    But though rather flash,
    He lacks my panache,
And *he* can't come eight times in a night.'

✳

There was a young girl of Gibraltar
Who was raped as she knelt at the altar.
    It really seems odd
    That a virtuous God
Should answer her prayers, and assault her.

＊

'Given faith,' sighed the Vicar of Deneham,
'From the lusts of the flesh we might wean 'em.
   But the human soul sighs
   For a nice pair of thighs
And a little of what lies between 'em.'

＊

   An indolent vicar of Bray
   Kept his wife in the family way,
     Till she grew more alert,
     Bought a vaginal squirt,
   And said to her spouse, 'Let us spray!'

＊

   There once was a chaplain of King's
   Whose mind dwelt on heavenly things,
     But his heart was on fire
     For a boy in the choir,
   With a bottom like jelly on springs.

＊

From the depths of the crypt at St Giles
Came a scream that resounded for miles.
   Said the vicar, 'Good gracious!
   Has Father Ignatius
Forgotten the bishop has piles?'

❋

Have you heard of the Bishop of Kew
Who preached with his vestments askew?
   A lady named Morgan
   Caught sight of his organ
And fainted away in her pew.

❋

There was a young lady of Devon
Who was raped in the garden by seven
   High Anglican priests
   (Lascivious beasts):
Of such is the kingdom of heaven.

❋

There once was a priest of Gibraltar
Who wrote dirty jokes in his psalter.
   An inhibited nun
   Who had read every one
Made a vow to be laid on his altar.

❋

A young novice priest of Lahore
Ogled nuns in the convent galore.
   He climbed in and defiled one
   Who proved such a wild one
He stayed to defile her some more.

❋

'Well, madam,' the bishop declared,
While the vicar just mumbled and stared,
   ' 'Twere better, perhaps,
   In the crypt or the apse,
Because sex in the nave must be shared.'

❋

Mused the deacon, in deepest dejection,
As he passed round the box for collection:
   'If it comes to the worst,
   Can a curate be cursed
Or a rector be wrecked by erection?'

❋

A Salvation lassie named Claire
Was having her first love-affair.
　　As she climbed into bed
　　She reverently said,
'I wish to be opened with prayer.'

❋

A renegade priest from Liberia,
Whose behaviour was clearly inferior,
　　Once did to a nun
　　What she longed to have done
And now she's a Mother Superior.

❋

When a lecherous curate of Leeds
Was discovered one day in the weeds
　　Astride a young nun,
　　He said, 'Christ this is fun!
Far better than telling one's beads.'

❋

There once was a nun whose divinity
Preserved her in perfect virginity,
　　Till a candle, her nemesis,
　　Caused parthenogenesis –
And she thinks herself one of the Trinity.

✳

There was a young fellow named Baker
Who seduced a vivacious young Quaker.
    And when he had done it
    She straightened her bonnet
And said, 'I give thanks to my Maker.'

✳

'The conception,' an archbishop said,
'Of a personal tempter is dead.'
    But a meek little curate
    Begged leave to demur; it
Was something he fought with in bed.

✳

A habit obscene and unsavory
Holds the Bishop of Wessex in slavery.
    With maniacal howls
    He deflowers young owls
Which he keeps in an underground aviary.

✳

But the prior of Dunstan St Just,
Cunsumed with erotical lust,
    Raped the bishop's prize fowls
    (His treasured young owls)
And a little green lizard, what bust

✳

There was a young curate of Buckingham,
Who was blamed by the girls for not fucking 'em.
    He said: 'Though my cock
    Is as hard as a rock,
Your cunts are too slack. Put a tuck in 'em.'

✳

There was a young lady called Alice
Who peed in a Catholic chalice.
    The padre agreed
    It was done out of need,
And not out of Protestant malice.

✳

There was a young priest from Madrid
Who looked with lewd eyes on a kid.
    He said, 'With great joy,
    I could bugger that boy.
I'll be damned if I don't!' And he did.

✳

Said the bishop one day to the abbott,
Whose instincts were just like a rabbit:
    'I know it's great fun
    To embrace a young nun –
But you mustn't get into the habit.'

*

A fervent young maid of Bermuda
Embraced all the doctrines of Buddha;
    But in six weeks, all told,
    She returned to the fold,
When the Anglican archbishop screwed her.

*

On a bridge sat the Bishop of Buckingham
Who was thinking of twats and of sucking them –
    And watching the stunts
    Of the cunts in the punts
And the tricks of the pricks that were
                                        fucking them.

❋

There was a young fellow named Sistall,
Who shot three old maids with a pistol.
  When 'twas known what he'd done,
  He was given a gun
By the unmarried curates of Bristol.

❋

There was young fellow of Sherborne,
Who would go to church in a turban:
  When they put him outside,
  He politely replied
That he thought their ideas were suburban.

❋

A prelate of very high station
Was impeached by a pious relation.
  He was found in a ditch
  With – I won't say a witch,
But a woman of no education.

❋

There was a young lady of Clun,
Who dressed herself up as a nun,
  But she could not disguise
  Her beautiful eyes
Or she would not have had so much fun.

✳

There was a young lass from Helvellyn
Who eloped with the Vicar of Welwyn.
　　But the local hotelwyn
　　The rear had a wellwyn:
And they never got wed, for they fellwyn.

✳

These verses, one can but surmise,
Were not meant for clerical eyes.
　　Should the Bishop and Dean
　　Find out what they mean
They ought to turn pink with surprise.

✳

And if, among Romish admirers,
They stimulate naughty desires,
　　Confess them, at least,
　　To your neighbourhood priest,
For the price of ten Ave Marias.

✳

There once was a Bishop of Bude
Who every so often got screwed.
　　He might have atoned
　　If he'd only got stoned,
But a Rev. getting screwed — well, that's lewd.

✳

The unfortunate Dean of South Herts
Was caught importuning some tarts;
　　His good wife was shocked
　　When the Dean was unfrocked:
For the first time she saw all his parts.

✳

The Reverend Henry Ward Beecher
Called a hen a most elegant creature.
　　The hen, pleased with that,
　　Laid an egg in his hat,
And thus did the hen reward Beecher.

✳

There once was a curate of Kew
Who kept a tom-cat in a pew.
　　He taught it to speak
　　Alphabetical Greek
But it never got further than μ.

✳

There was a young curate of Minster,
Who admonished a giddy young spinster.
　　For she used, on the ice,
　　Words not at all nice
When he, at a turn, slid against her.

✻

The Reverend Mr Uprightly
Was cuckolded daily and nightly.
    He murmured, 'Dear, dear!
    I would fain interfere
If I knew how to do it politely.'

✻

There was a young lady called Tessa
A quite unrepentant transgressor;
    When sent to the priest
    The lewd little beast
Began to undress her confessor.

✻

There once was a Vicar of Horsham
Who always took every precaution,
    Till one Ermyntrude
    Let a stray sperm intrude
And that was a case for abortion.

✻

The robes of the Vicar of Cheltenham
Gave him pleasure whenever he knelt in 'em.
    But they got rather hot
    When he wore them a lot,
And the Vicar of Cheltenham smelt in 'em.

✳

There once was a vicar of Clymping
Who earned tons of money from pimping.
  When his bishop asked why,
  He replied with a sigh:
'Well, you can't have a man of God skimping.'

✳

Our vicar's an absolute duck –
But just now, he's down on his luck:
  At the Sunday School treat
  He tripped over his feet,
And all of us heard him say, 'Now children, let
                us stand up and say Grace.'

✳

There once was an innocent Quaker
Who fell for a baker called Dacre.
  Five minutes of lovin'
  Put a bun in her oven,
And made the young baker forsake her.

✳

There was a young girl with a feeling
That if she spent long enough kneeling
  She'd feel the reception
  Of the immaculate conception.
(Note: The man under the bed came
                from Ealing.)

✳

There were two ladies of Birmingham,
I know a sad story concerningham:
   They stuck needles and pins
   In the right reverend shins
Of the bishop engaged in confirmingham.

✳

A bibulous Bishop of Norwich
Lived mainly on whisky and porridge.
   He liked to top up
   His communion cup
With Pimms No. 1, port and borage.

✳

An indolent vicar of Bray
His roses allowed to decay;
　　His wife, more alert,
　　Bought a powerful squirt
And said to her spouse, 'Let us spray.'

✳

A young nun who wrote verse in her diary,
That was terribly torrid and fiery,
　　Once left it behind
　　For the abbess to find –
Now she isn't allowed in the priory.

✳

A dean who was rather a prude
Thus addressed a sunbather at Bude:
　　'Excuse me, but – er, miss –
　　So much epidermis
Makes me feel that the cloth should intrude.'

✳

There once was a fellow called Grover
Who bowled seven wides in an over,
　　Which had never been done
　　By an archdeacon's son
On Tuesday, in August, at Dover.

Cynical,
Practical
&
Commonsensical

If you want a proud foe to 'make tracks' –
If you'd melt a rich uncle in wax –
    You've but to look in
    On our resident djinn,
Number seventy, Simmery Axe . . .

✳

An important young man from Quebec
Had to welcome the Duchess of Teck,
    So he bought for a dollar
    A very high collar
To save himself washing his neck.

✳

As they fished his old plane from the sea,
The inventor just chortled with glee.
    'I shall build,' and he laughed,
    'A submarine craft,
And perhaps it will fly, we shall see.'

✳

There was a young lady of Venice
Who used hard-boiled eggs to play tennis.
    People said, 'That is wrong.'
    She replied, 'Go along!
You don't know how prolific my hen is.'

❋

There was a young lady of Crete,
Who was so exceedingly neat:
    When she got out of bed
    She stood on her head
To make sure of not soiling her feet.

❋

There was an old woman of Clewer
Who was riding a bike, and it threw her.
    A butcher came by
    And said, 'Missus, don't cry,'
And fixed her back on, with a skewer.

❋

A Turk named Abdullah Ben Barum
Had sixty-five wives in his harem.
    When his favourite horse died,
    'Mighty Allah!' he cried,
'Take a few of my wives – I can spare 'em.'

❋

There was a young lady of Bandon
Whose feet were too narrow to stand on;
    So she stood on her head,
    'For my motto,' she said,
'Has always been *Nil desperandum*.'

✳

There once was a baby of yore
Whose parents found it a bore,
    And being afraid
    It might be mislaid
They stored it away in a drawer.

✳

There was a most finicky lass,
Who always wore panties of brass.
    When they asked, 'Don't they chafe?'
    She said, 'Yes, but I'm safe
From prickles and pins in the grass.'

✳

There was a young man from Darjeeling
Who got on a bus bound for Ealing.
    It said at the door,
    'Don't spit on the floor';
So he carefully spat on the ceiling.

✳

When twins came, their father, Dan Dunn,
Gave Edward as name to each son.
    When folks cried, 'Absurd!'
    He replied, 'Ain't you heard
That two Eds are better than one?'

❋

An impish young fellow named James
Had a passion for idiot games.
　　He lighted the hair
　　Of his lady's affair,
And laughed as she peed out the flames.

❋

There was an old lady who said,
When she found a thief under her bed,
　　'So near to the floor,
　　And so close to the door!
I'm afraid you'll catch cold in your head.'

❋

Said a salty old skipper of Wales,
'Number One, it's all right to chew nails;
　　It impresses the crew,
　　It impresses me too:
But stop spitting holes in the sails.'

❋

There was a young golfer at Troon
Who always played golf with a spoon.
　　'It's handy,' said he,
　　'For the brandy, you see,
Should anyone happen to swoon.'

✳

A waitress on day-shift at Schraffts
Has a couple of interesting craffts.
   She's exceedingly able
   At upsetting the table
And screwing in dumb-waiter schaffts.

✳

If you find for your verse there's no call,
And you can't afford paper at all,
   For the poet true born,
   However forlorn,
There's always the lavatory wall.

❋

A young lass on a yacht in Glandore,
So tired she could do it no more;
   'But I'm willing to try
   So where shall I lie?
On the deck, on the sail, or the floor?'

❋

There once was a spinster of Ealing,
Endowed with such delicate feeling,
   That she thought that a chair
   Should not have its legs bare,
So she kept her eyes fixed on the ceiling.

❋

There was an old maid, name of Rood,
Who was such an absolute prude,
   That she pulled down the blind
   When changing her mind
Lest libidinous eyes should intrude.

❋

You may not believe me, and yet,
Old girls are the very best bet.
   They don't yell, tell or swell,
   And they screw hard as hell
For it may be the last one they'll get!

❋

There was a young lady called Wilde
Who kept herself quite undefiled
   By thinking of Jesus,
   Contagious diseases,
And the bother of having a child.

❋

There was a young girl from Bordeaux
Whose mother said, 'Always say "No".'
   But the girl said 'No' after
   The fun when, with laughter,
She'd screwed her good friend Pierrot.

❋

A boy scout was having his fill
Of a brownie's sweet charms up a hill.
   'We're prepared; yes, of course,'
   Said scoutmistress Gorse,
'My girl scouts are all on the pill.'

❋

Said an innocent girlie named Shelley
As her man rolled her on to her belly:
   'This is not the position
   For human coition –
And why the petroleum jelly?'

✳

'It's Pony Express,' said Miss Pound:
'A wonderful game that we've found;
    Like Post Office,' she said,
    'But you play it in bed,
And there's a little more horsing around.'

✳

A lassie from wee Ballachulish
Observed, 'Och, virginity's foolish;
    When a lad makes a try,
    To say ought but "Aye!"
Is stubborn, pig-headed and mulish.'

✳

There was a young lady of Clewer
Who was riding a bike and it threw her.
    A man saw her there
    With her legs in the air,
And seized the occasion to screw her.

✳

Said a maid: 'I will marry for lucre,'
And her scandalised ma almost shucre;
    But when the chance came,
    And she told the old dame,
I notice she didn't rebucre.

❊

There was a young lady of Dover,
Whose passion was such that it drove her
 To cry, when you came,
 'Oh dear! What a shame!
Well, now we shall have to start over.'

❊

Said Miss Farrow, on one of her larks,
'Sex is more fun in bed than in parks.
 You feel more at ease;
 Your butt doesn't freeze
And passers-by don't make remarks.'

✳

The sex-drive of old man McGill
Gives fortunate ladies a thrill.
   They say his technique
   Is delightful, unique:
And involves an electrical drill!

✳

A candid young lady named Tudor
Remarked to the chap who'd just screwed her,
   'After dildoes, dilators
   And electric vibrators,
The real thing feels like an intruder.'

✳

A young window-cleaner named Luigi
Was screwing a lady from Fiji.
   When she broke into sweat
   He said, 'Hold on, my pet,'
And squeezed off the sweat with his squeegee.

✳

There was a young harlot from Kew
Who filled her vagina with glue.
   Said she, with a grin,
   'If they pay to get in,
They'll pay to get out of it, too.'

✳

A pimp toured his whore through ten nations,
Selling sundry and various sexations,
   And when asked his position,
   Answered, 'Pushing coition –
I handle her pubic relations.'

✳

A starry-eyed starlet named Charlotte
Said, 'Hollywood! Home of the harlot!
   Where cute split-tail bitches
   Take quick rides to riches,
If their sins are sufficiently scarlet.'

✳

The erotic desires of Miss Myers
Required a great many suppliers.
   When she found, in late years,
   Far too few volunteers,
She brought in a pimp, who got buyers.

✳

A naked young tart named Roselle
Walked the streets while ringing a bell;
   When asked why she rang it,
   She answered, 'God, dang it!
Can't you see I have something to sell?'

❋

A tired young trollop of Nome
Was worn out from her toes to her dome.
   Eight miners came screwing,
   But she said, 'Nothing doing;
One of you has to go home!'

❋

I remarked to the mermaid, 'My dear,
I have pondered on this for a year:
   As it's fruitless to hunt
   For a cunt in your front,
May I offer a prick up your ear?'

❋

There was a young party of Bicester
Who wanted to bugger his sister,
   But not liking dirt
   He purchased a squirt
and rinsed out the part with a clyster.

❋

Have you heard of the widow O'Reilly
Who esteemed her late husband so highly
   That, in spite of the scandal,
   Her umbrella handle
Was made of his *membrum virile*?

✳

There was a young woman of Croft
Who played with herself in a loft,
　　Having reasoned that candles
　　Could never cause scandals,
Besides which they did not go soft.

✳

There was a young lady of Harrow
Who complained that her cunt was too narrow,
　　For times without number
　　She would use a cucumber,
But could not encompass a marrow.

❋

A sailor who slept in the sun
Woke to find his fly-buttons undone.
 He remarked with a smile,
 'By Jove, a sundial –
And now it's a quarter past one!'

❋

A mechanical marvel was Bill,
He'd a tool that was shaped like a quill;
 With this fabulous dink
 He could squirt purple ink
And decorate lampshades at will.

❋

There once was a Queen of Bulgaria
Whose bush had grown hairier and hairier,
 Till a prince from Peru
 Who came up for a screw
Had to hunt for her cunt with a terrier.

❋

Every time Lady Lowbodice swoons,
Her bubbies pop out like balloons;
 But her butler stands by
 With hauteur in his eye
And lifts them back in with warm spoons.

❋

There was a young lady of Spain
Who took down her pants on the train.
   There was a young porter
   Saw more than he orter
And asked her to do it again.

❋

Said a luscious young lady called Wade,
On a beach with her charms all displayed:
   'It's so hot in the sun,
   Perhaps rape would be fun,
At least that would give me some shade.'

✻

Petunia, the prude of Mount Hood,
Devised an odd object of wood
    Which, employed on hot nights,
    Gave her carnal delights
Far beyond what the average man could.

✻

It somehow seems highly ironical
That a Londoner laid Miss McGonagal,
    And having no rubber
    The sex-crazy lubber
Whipped out and inserted his monocle!

✻

There was a young man from Calcutta
Who was heard in his beard to mutter,
    'If her Bartholin glands
    Don't respond to my hands,
I'm afraid I shall have to use butter.'

✻

All winter a eunuch from Munich
Went out wearing only his tunic;
    Folk said, 'You've a cough:
    You'll freeze your balls off!'
Said he, 'I'm already a eunuch.'

✳

A geologist named Dr Robb
Was perturbed by his thingamybob,
   So he took up his pick
   And whanged off his wick,
And calmly went on with his job.

✳

There was a young girl from Madrid
Who learned she was having a kid.
   By holding her water
   Two months and a quarter
She drowned the poor bastard, she did.

✳

There was a young girl from Sofia
Who succumbed to her lover's desire.
   She said, 'Sure, it's a sin;
   But now that it's in,
Could you shove it a little bit higher?'

✳

There was a young girl of La Plata
Who was widely renowned as a farter.
   Her deafening reports
   At the Argentine Sports
Made her much in demand as a starter.

*

There was a crusader from Parma
Who lovingly fondled a charmer.
   Said the maiden demure:
    'You'll excuse me, I'm sure,
But I wish you would take off your armour.'

*

A mouse in her room woke Miss Dowd;
She was frightened, it must be allowed.
   Then a happy thought hit her:
    To scare off the critter,
She knelt on the floor and meeowed.

*

'Far dearer to me than my treasure,'
Miss Guggenheim said, 'is my leisure;
   For then I can screw
    The whole Harvard crew –
They're slow, but it lengthens the pleasure.'

*

There was a young girl of Shanghai
Who was so exceedingly shy
   That undressing at night
    She turned out the light
For fear of the All-Seeing Eye.

❋

'The beds are all full,' said Miranda
To her beau, with commendable candour,
  'And our antique chaise longue
  Is not very strong –
So why don't we try the verandah?'

❋

On the chest of a barmaid in Sale
Was tattooed all the prices of ale,
  And on her behind
  For the sake of the blind
Was the same list of prices in Braille.

❋

A lecherous student from Leeds
One day had to pay for misdeeds.
    When a man with a gun
    Said: 'You'll marry her, son,
You must harvest when you sow the seeds.'

❋

There was a tiresome young man in Bay Shore;
When his fiancée cried, 'I adore
    The beautiful sea!'
    He replied, 'I agree
It's pretty. But what is it for?'

❋

There was a young woman of Aenos
Who came to our party as Venus.
    We told her how rude
    'Twas to come there quite nude,
And we brought her a leaf from the green-h'us.

❋

A girl who weighed many an oz.
Used language I dare not pronoz.
    When a fellow unkind
    Pulled her chair out behind
Just to see (so he said) if she'd boz.

Economical, Financial

&

Mercatorial

There was an old miser of Reading,
Had a house, with a yard, with a shed in;
   'Twas meant for a cow,
   But so small that I vow
The poor creature could scarce get its head in.

✳

There was an old maid of Genoa,
And I blush when I think what Iowa.
   She's gone to her rest,
   And it's all for the best,
Otherwise I would borrow Samoa.

✳

There's a clever old miser who tries
Every method to e–con–omise.
   He said with a wink,
   'I save gallons of ink
By simply not dotting my i's.'

✳

There once was a young girl named Jeanie
Whose dad was a terrible meanie:
   He fashioned a latch
   And a hatch for her snatch –
She could only be had by Houdini.

✳

An obstinate lady of Leicester
Wouldn't marry her swain, though
                              he preicester.
   For his income, I fear,
   Was a hundred a year,
On which he could never have dreicester.

✳

There was a young Scot in Madrid
Who got fifty-five fucks for a quid.
   When they said, 'Are you faint?'
   He replied, 'No, I ain't,
But I don't feel as good as I did.'

✳

There was a young Scotsman named Dave
Who kept a dead whore in a cave.
   He said, 'I admit
   I'm a bit of a shit,
But think of the money I save!'

✳

There once was a pro from Madrid,
Whose minimum charge was a quid.
   Came along an Italian,
   With balls like a stallion,
Said he'd do it for nothing, and did.

✳

Said a charming young lady of Padua,
'A peso! Why, sir, what a cadua!'
     He said, lifting his hat,
     'You ain't even worth that.
However, I'm glad to have hadua.'

✳

A fallen young lady of fashion
Gave vent to all sorts of base passion.
     Was she scorned? She was not,
     For her ways brought a lot
Of highly respectable cash in.

✳

An awful old bounder, McGee,
Used to think he could dip his wick free.
     But a harlot named Charlotte
     Remarked with a snarl, 'It
Is business, not pleasure, with me.'

✳

An indolent lass from Iraq
Spent a great deal of time in the sack.
     She could earn a month's pay
     In a night and a day
Without once getting up off her back.

❋

A businesslike harlot named Draper
Once tried an unusual caper.
    What made it so nice
    Was you got it half-price
If you brought in her ad from the paper.

❋

'Give in to your filthy desires?
I should think not!' cried haughty Miss Myers.
    'The only thing free
    That that part does is pee;
For the other, I've plenty of buyers.'

❋

There was an old girl of Kilkenny
Whose usual charge was a penny.
    For half of that sum
    You might fondle her bum:
A source of amusement to many.

❋

The tax-paying whores of the nation
Sent Congress a large delegation
    To convince those old fools
    Their professional tools
Were subject to depreciation.

❋

There was an old whore named McGee
Who was just the right sort for a spree.
  She said, 'For a fuck,
  I charge half a buck,
And throw in the asshole for free.'

❋

That elegant gigolo, Price,
Remarked, 'Now, it *may* be a vice,
  But one thing I know,
  This dancing for dough
Is something exceedingly nice.'

❋

A shiftless young fellow of Kent
Had his wife fuck the landlord for rent;
  But as she grew older,
  The landlord grew colder,
And now they live out in a tent.

❋

I think I must speak to my wife:
She's been giving free tail to old Fife.
  It isn't the screwing
  I mind the bitch doing,
It's the 'free' part that's causing the strife!

✳

For widower – wanted – housekeeper,
Not too bloody refined, a light sleeper;
   When employer's inclined,
   Must be game for a grind,
Pay generous, mind, but can't keep her.

✳

There was a young fellow from Yale
Whose face was exceedingly pale.
   He spent his vacation
   In self-masturbation
Because of the high price of tail.

✳

There once was a lady named Mabel,
So ready, so willing, so able,
   And so full of spice
   She could name her own price –
Now Mabel's all wrapped up in sable.

✳

There once was a maid with such graces
That her curves cried aloud for
embraces.
   'You look,' said McGee,
   'Like a million to me
Invested in all the right places.'

❋

It seems I impregnated Marge,
So I do rather feel, by and large,
    Some dough should be tendered
    For services rendered,
But I can't quite decide what to charge.

❋

On a picnic a Scot named McFee
Was stung in the balls by a bee.
    He made oodles of money
    By oozing pure honey
Each time he attempted to pee.

❋

There was a young man of Montrose,
Who had pockets in none of his clothes.
    When asked by his lass
    Where he carried his brass,
He said: 'Darling, I pay through the nose.'

❋

There was a young lady from Dorset
Who went to a pennyworth closet.
    But when she got there
    She could only puff air –
That wasn't a pennyworth, was it?

✳

There was an old barber from Hythe
Who shaved stubbly chins with a scythe.
　　He said: 'It comes cheaper
　　Than using a reaper,
Though it does make the customers writhe.'

✳

An industrious young obstetrician
Conceived his financial position
　　To depend upon beauty
　　And husbandly duty,
Plus determined and endless coition.

✳

There was a young cashier of Calais
Whose accounts when reviewed wouldn't talais.
  But his chief smelled a rat
  When he furnished a flat
And was seen every night at the balais.

✳

There was a young lady called Valerie
Who started to count every calorie.
  Said her boss in disgust,
  'If you lose half your bust
Then you're worth only half of your salary.'

✳

There was a young harlot named Bunny
Whose kisses were sweeter than honey;
  Her callers galore
  Would line up at her door
To take turns in paying her money.

✳

In Wall Street a girl named Irene
Made an offering somewhat obscene:
  She stripped herself bare
  And offered a share
To Merrill Lynch, Pierce, Fenner and Beane.

Gastronomical,
Alcoholical
&
Indigestible

There was an old person of Florence
Who held mutton chops in abhorrence;
    He purchased a bustard,
    And fried him in mustard,
Which choked that old person of Florence.

＊

There was an old man of Thermopylae
Who never did anything properly;
    But they said, 'If you choose
    To boil eggs in your shoes,
You shall never remain in Thermopylae.'

＊

There was an old person of Ewell
Who chiefly subsisted on gruel;
    But to make it more nice
    He inserted some mice,
Which refreshed that old person of Ewell.

＊

There was an old man of the coast
Who placidly sat on a post;
    But when it was cold
    He relinquished his hold
And called for some hot buttered toast.

✳

There was an old person of Dean
Who dined on one pea and one bean;
    For he said, 'More than that
      Would make me too fat,'
That cautious old person of Dean.

✳

There was a professor named Chesterton
Who went for a walk with his best shirt on.
   Being hungry, he ate it,
   But lived to regret it,
For he ruined for life his digestion.

✳

A drunken old tar from St Clements,
To ward off the scurvy sucked lemons.
   'With my health unimpaired
   I'll have time,' he declared,
'To die of delirium tremens.'

✳

A discerning person from Swaffham
Would seek out real ales, and then quaff 'em;
   The problem that played
   On the mind of the trade
Lay in getting the cost of them off him.

✳

There was a co-ed of Cayenne
Who ate onions, blue cheese and sen-sen;
  Till a bad fright one day
  Took her breath quite away,
And we hope she won't find it again.

✳

To his wife said a grumbler named Dutton,
'I'm a gourmet, I am, not a glutton.
  For ham, jam or lamb,
  I don't give a damn,
So come on, let's return to our mutton.'

✳

A cannibal bold of Penzance
Ate an uncle and two of his aunts,
  A cow and her calf,
  An ox and a half,
And now he can't button his pants.

✳

There was an old lady of Brooking
Who had a great genius for cooking.
  She could bake sixty pies,
  All quite the same size,
And tell which was which without looking

✳

There's a lady in Kalamazoo
Who first bites her oysters in two;
    She has a misgiving,
    Should any be living,
They'd raise such a hullabaloo.

✳

The mouth of a glutton named Moto
Was the size that no organ should grow to.
    It could take in with ease
    Six carrots, ten peas,
And a whole baked potato *in toto*.

✳

When Daddy and Mum got quite plastered,
And their shame had been thoroughly
                        mastered,
    They told their boy Harry,
    'Son, we never did marry;
But don't tell the neighbours, you bastard.'

✳

There once was a bonnie Scotch laddie
Who said as he put on his plaidie,
    'I've just had a dish
    O' unco' guid fish.'
What had he had? Had he had haddie?

✳

A Korean whose home was in Seoul
Had notions uncommonly droll;
    He'd get himself stewed
    And pose in the nude
On top of a telegraph pole.

✳

There was a young man from Tacoma
Whose breath had a whiskey aroma;
    So to alter the smell
    He swallowed Chanel
And went off in a heavenly coma.

✳

The kings of Peru were the Incas,
Who were known far and wide as great drincas;
    They worshipped the sun,
    And had lots of fun,
But the peons all thought them great stincas.

✳

A bibulous chap from Duquesne
Drank a whole jeroboam of champagne.
    Said he, with a laugh
    As he quaffed the last quaff,
'I tried to get drunk, but in vain!'

*

Well, if it's a sin to like Guinness,
Then that I admit's what my sin is.
    I like it with fizz,
    Or just as it is,
And it's much better for me than gin is.

*

A Turk by the name of Haroun
Ate whisky by means of a spoon.
    When someone asked, 'Why?'
    He gave this reply,
'To drink is forbidden, you loon!'

*

A glutton from Bingen-am-Rhein
Was asked at what hour he would dine.
    He replied, 'At eleven,
    At three, five and seven,
And eight; and a quarter to nine.'

*

There was a young person named Tate
Took a girl out to eat at 8.08;
    But I will not relate
    What Tate and his date
Ate, tête-à-tête, at 8.08.

❋

This shortage of help has produced
More kitchen-wise males than it used –
   Like that man of gallantry
   Who, leaving the pantry,
Remarked, 'Well, my cook is well goosed!'

✳

There was an old man of Peru
Who dreamt he was eating his shoe.
   He woke in the night
   In a terrible fright
And found it was perfectly true.

✳

There once was a lady of Ryde
Who ate cider apples, and died;
   Inside the lamented
   The apples fermented
To cider inside her inside.

✳

There was a young fellow named Sydney,
Who drank till he ruined his kidney.
   It shrivelled and shrank,
   As he sat there and drank,
But he had a good time at it, didn't he?

✳

An effeminate fellow from Lincoln
One night did some serious drincoln,
   Met a gal, now his wife,
   Learned the true facts of life,
And blesses the day he got stincoln.

*

There was a young lady of Munich
Whose appetite simply was unich.
   She contentedly cooed,
    'There's nothing like food,'
As she let out a tuck in her tunich.

*

When a certain young woman named Terry
Got drunk on a small sip of sherry,
   She'd insist upon games
   With embarrassing names
Not in any refined dictionary.

*

There was a young lady of Kent
Who said that she knew what it meant
   When men asked her to dine,
   Gave her cocktails, and wine;
She knew what it meant: but she went!

*

There was a young girl named McKnight
Who got drunk with her boyfriend one night.
   She came to in bed
   With a split maidenhead –
That's the last time she ever was tight.

❋

At last I've seduced the au pair –
On steak and a chocolate eclair,
    Some peas and some chips,
    Three Miracle Whips
And a carafe of *vin ordinaire*!

❋

There was an old lady of Troy
Who invented a new sort of joy:
    She sugared her quim
    And frosted the rim,
And then had it sucked by a boy.

❋

Some night when you're drunk on Dutch Bols
Try changing the usual roles.
    The backward position
    Is nice for coition
And offers the choice of two holes.

❋

When you think of the hosts without no.
Who are slain by the deadly cuco.
    Its quite a mistake
    Of such food to partake:
It results in a permanent slo.

❉

There was an old man of Dundee
Who came home as drunk as can be;
    He wound up the clock
    With the end of his cock,
And buggered his wife with the key.

❉

To evade paternity, Mick
Said, 'Anal or oral, you pick.
    Try sucking my cock –
    It's like Blackpool rock.
Oh, come on, just give it a lick.'

❉

There was a young lady of Malta
Who strangled her aunt with a halter.
    She said, 'I won't bury her;
    She'll do for my terrier.
She'll keep for a month if I salt her.'

❉

A certain young gourmet of Crediton
Took some *pâté de foie gras* and spread it on
    A chocolate biscuit,
    Then murmured, 'I'll risk it.'
His tomb bears the date that he said it on

*

There was once a schoolboy, named Hannibal,
Who won local fame as a cannibal
   By eating his mother,
   His father, his brother
And his two sisters, Gertrude and Annabel.

*

There was a young lady named Sue
Who preferred a stiff drink to a screw.
   But one leads to the other,
   And now she's a mother –
Let this be a lesson to you.

*

There was a young chappie named
Cholmondeley
Who always at dinner sat dolmondeley.
   His fair partner said
   As he crumbled his bread:
'Dear me! You behave very rolmondeley.'

*

A Classical man from Victoria,
In a post-alcoholic euphoria,
   Was discovered one day
   In a club for the gay
Immersed in an *Ars Amatoria*.

❋

There once was a very old gnu
Who was used by a chef in some stew.
   He should have been told
   The gnu was too old:
For stews, only new gnus will do.

❋

There was a young lady called Brigid
Whose sex life was apt to be frigid.
   So they used to begin
   With a bottle of gin
Till the boyfriend (not Brigid) was rigid.

❋

A venturesome three-week-old chamois;
Strayed off in the woods from his mamois;
   He might have been dead
   But some picknickers fed
Him with sandwiches, milk and salamois.

❋

There was a young weaver from Wapping
Who thought his first whisky was topping;
   He swallowed it down
   With a dubious frown
And hiccuped six weeks without stopping.

❋

There was a young woman named Riley
Who valued old candle-ends highly;
    When no one was looking
    She used them for cooking.
'It's wicked to taste,' she said dryly.

❋

There was a young man of Rheims,
Who was subject to having wet dreams;
    He bottled a dozen,
    To send to his cousin,
And labelled them 'chocolate creams'.

❋

A cheese that was aged and grey
Was walking and talking one day;
    Said the cheese, 'Kindly note
    My mama was a goat –
And I'm made out of curds, by the whey.'

Heterosexual,
Universal
&
Disgraceful

There was a young girl of Aberystwyth
Who took grain to the mill to make grist
with;
  The miller's son Jack
  Laid her on her back
And united the organs they pissed with.

✳

Connoisseurs of coition aver
That the best British girls never stir.
  This condition in Persia
  Is known as inertia:
It depends what response you prefer.

✳

There was a young man of Belgrade
Who planned to seduce a fair maid;
  And as it befell
  He suceeded quite well,
So the maid, like the plan, was deep-laid.

✳

There was a young lady of station,
'I love man!' was her exclamation;
    But when men cried: 'You flatter!'
    She replied: 'Oh, no matter!'
Isle of Man is the explanation.

✻

There was a young woman who lay
With her legs wide apart in the hay;
   Then, calling a ploughman,
    She said: 'Do it now, man!
Don't wait till your hair has turned grey!'

✻

There was a young lady of Exeter,
So pretty that men craned their nexeter.
   One was even so brave
    As to take out and wave
The distinguishing mark of his sexeter.

✻

An innocent maiden of Gloucester
Fell in love with a coucester named Foucester;
   She met him in Leicester,
    Where he merely careicester,
Then the hard-headed coucester just loucester.

✻

A lady, an expert on skis,
Went out with a man who said, 'Plis,
   On the next precipice,
    Will you give me a kice?'
She said, 'Quick, before somebody sis!'

✳

Arabella's a terrible prude;
She says, 'Men are beasts. Men are lewd.
  A girl has to watch
  Or their hand's in her crotch,
And the next thing she knows, she is screwed.'

✳

    As Bradley is said to have said,
    'If I think that I'm lying in bed
      With this girl that I feel
      And can touch, is it real?
    Or just going on in my head?'

✳

There was a young lady from Powys,
Who asked of her lover, 'Just howys
  It possible for you
  To perform as you do?'
Quoth he, 'An amalgam of ability and prowys.'

✳

    In his youth our old friend Boccaccio
    Was having a girl on a patio;
      When it came to the twat
      She wasn't so hot,
    But, boy, was she good at fellatio!

*

There once was a couple named Mound
Whose sexual control was profound:
    When engaged in coition,
    They had the ambition
To study the *Cantos* of Pound.

*

A young man by a girl was desired,
To give her the thrills she required;
    But he died of old age
    Ere his cock cold assuage
The volcanic desires it inspired.

*

A desperate spinster from Clare
Once knelt in the moonlight all bare
    And prayed to her God
    For a romp on the sod –
A passer-by answered her prayer.

*

An astonished ex-virgin named Howard
Remarked, after being deflowered,
    'I knew that connection
    Was made in that section,
But not that it's so darn high-powered.'

❊

'Yes, of course,' said a girl from Latrop,
'But it's hard to know quite where to stop:
   A boy lifts your slip
   Then you hear him unzip,
Then what do you do? Call a cop?'

❊

There was a young lady named Smith
Whose virtue was mostly a myth.
   She said, 'Try as I can,
   I can't find a man
Whom it's fun to be virtuous with.'

❊

There was a young lady of Slough
Who said that she didn't know how –
   Till a young fellow caught her
   And jolly well taught her,
And she lodges in Pimlico now.

❊

An inquisitive virgin named Dora
Whose boy was beginning to bore her:
   'Do you mean birds and bees
   Go through antics like these
To provide us with flora and fauna?'

✳

There was a young girl with a bust
Which aroused a French cavalier's lust.
    She was since heard to say,
    About midnight, '*Touché!*
I didn't quite parry that thrust!'

✳

A rascal, far gone in treachery,
Lured maids to their doom with his lechery;
    He invited them in
    For the purpose of sin,
Though he said 'twas to look at his etchery.

✳

I met a lewd nude in Bermuda
Who thought she was shrewd: I was shrewder;
    She thought it quite crude
    To be wooed in the nude –
I pursued her, subdued her, and screwed her.

✳

Said a very attractive young Haitian,
'Please begin with a gentle palpation.
    If you do as I say
    In the way of foreplay,
Why, who knows? There may be fornication.'

✳

I dislike all this crude notoriety
That I'm getting for my impropriety;
    All that I ever do
    Is what girls ask me to –
I admit, I get lots of variety.

✳

A girl who was touring Zambesi
Said, 'Attracting the men is quite easy:
    I don't wear any pants
    And, at every chance,
I stand where it's frightfully breezy.'

✳

Said a guy to his girlfriend, 'Virginia,
For ages I've courted to win ya.
    Now my point of frustration
    Has reached saturation –
This evening I gotta get in ya!'

✳

Breathed a tender young man from Australia,
'My darling, please let me unveilia,
    And then, O my own,
    If you'll kindly lie prone,
I'll endeavour, my sweet, to impaleia.'

✳

A self-centred young fellow named
Newcombe,
Who seduced many girls but made few come,
    Said, 'The pleasures of tail
    Were ordained for the male.
I've had mine. Do I care whether you come?'

✳

An insatiable satyr named Frazer
Is known as a wild woman-chaser.
    He's the main cause of myriads
    Of overdue periods,
For to him 'rubber' means an eraser.

❋

There was a young couple from Florida,
Whose passion grew steadily torrider;
   They had planned to sin
   At a room in the inn,
But, impatient, they screwed in the corridor.

❋

Said a certain old earl whom I knew,
'I've been struck from the rolls of *Who's Who*,
   Just because I was found
   Lying prone on the ground
     With the housemaid, and very nice too!'

❋

There was a young man of Eau Claire
Enjoying his girl on the stair.
   At the forty-fourth stroke
   The bannister broke,
And he finished her off in mid-air.

❋

My boy, if you like to have fun;
If you take all the girls one by one
   And when reaching four score
   Still don't find it a bore –
Why then, you're a hero, my son,

✳

'It is no use,' said Lady Maude Hoare,
'I can't concentrate any more.
    You're all in a sweat,
    And the sheets are quite wet,
And just look at the time: half-past four!'

✳

There was a young man from the War Office
Who got into bed with a whore of his.
    She slipped off her drawers
    With many a pause
But the chap from the War Office tore off his.

✳

'Austerity now is the fashion,'
Remarked a young lady with passion.
    Then she glanced at the bed
    And quietly said,
'But there's one thing that no one can ration.'

✳

The wife of a chronic crusader
Took on every man who waylaid her;
    Till the amorous itch
    Of this popular bitch
So annoyed the crusader he spayed her.

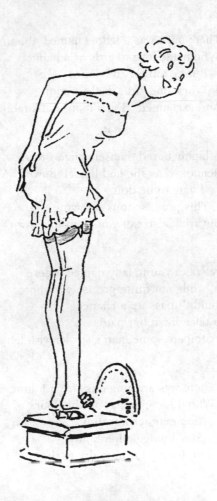

✳

There once was a fellow named Abbott
Who made love to girls as a habit;
    But he ran for the door
    When one girl asked for more,
And exclaimed, 'I'm a man, not a rabbit.'

✳

A highly bored damsel called Brown,
Remarked as she laid herself down:
    'I hate to be doing
    This promiscuous screwing,
But what else can you *do* in this town?'

✳

There was a young lady named Moore
Who, while not quite precisely a whore,
    Couldn't pass up a chance
    To take down her pants
And compare some man's stroke with her bore.

✳

There was a young miss from Johore
Who'd lie on a mat on the floor,
    In a manner uncanny
    She'd wriggle her fanny,
And drain your nuts dry to the core.

✳

There was a young plumber of Leigh
Who was plumbing a maid by the sea.
   Said the maid, 'Cease your plumbing:
   I think someone's coming!'
Said the plumber, still plumbing, 'It's me!'

✳

With his penis in turgid erection,
And aimed at woman's mid-section,
   Man looks most uncouth
   In that moment of truth
But she sheathes it with loving affection.

✳

A book and a jug and a dame,
And a nice cosy nook for the same –
   'And I don't care a damn,'
   Said Omar Khayyam,
'What you say. It's a great little game.'

✳

There was a young lady named Gay
Who was asked to make love in the hay.
   She jumped at the chance
   And took off her pants:
She was tickled to try it that way.

*

There once was a lady from Arden
Who sucked off a man in a garden.
   He said, 'My dear Flo,
   Where does all that stuff go?'
And she said – swallowing hard – 'I beg pardon?'

*

There is a young woman from Venice,
A regular sexual menace –
   For she'll hop from one boy
   To another with joy,
Like the ball in a fast game of tennis.

*

There was a young lady from Leicester
Who allowed the young men to molest her.
   For a kiss and a squeeze
   She would open her knees;
And she'd strip to the buff if they pressed her.

*

There's a luscious young charmer named Carmen
Who fucks for bums, boxers and barmen.
   Says she, 'The effete
   Have more brains but less meat.
I prefer hairy fellows who *are* men!'

✳

A notorious whore named Miss Hearst
In the weakness of men is well-versed;
  Reads a sign over the head
  Of her well-rumpled bed:
'The customer always comes first.'

✳

There was a young farmer of Nantes
Whose conduct was gay and gallant,
  For he fucked all his dozens
  Of nieces and cousins,
In addition, of course, to his aunt.

✳

There was a young man from Natal
And Sue was the name of his gal.
  He went out one day
  For a rather long way –
In fact, right up Sue'z Canal.

✳

An astonished young lady named Bissell
Let out a lascivious whistle
  When her boyfriend stripped nude.
  He remarked, 'Though it's crude,
Please observe that it's muscle, not missile!'

✳

There was a young lady of Chester
Who fell in love with a jester.
    Though her breath came out hotly
    At the sight of his motley,
It was really his wand that impressed her.

✳

Said a fair-headed maiden of Klondike:
'Of you I'm exceedingly fond, Ike.
    To prove I adore you,
    I'll dye, darling, for you,
And be a brunette, not a blonde, Ike.'

✳

There was a young man of Natal,
Who was having a Hottentot gal.
    She said: 'Oh, you sluggard!'
    He said: 'You be buggered!
I like to fuck slow, and I shall.'

✳

There was a young fellow named Phil
Who was screwing a girl, as boys will.
    She had a girl's knack
    Of screwing right back:
The instinct's not easy to kill.

❋

There was a young lady of Ealing
And her lover before her was kneeling.
    Said she, 'Dearest Jim,
    Take you hand off my quim;
I much prefer fucking to feeling.'

❋

When Dick made a young lady from Clare,
He was the very first one to get there.
    She said, 'Copulation
    Can result in gestation,
But gosh, now you're there, I don't care.'

❋

There was a young lady of Joppa
Who came a society cropper;
    She went to Ostend
    With a gentleman friend –
The rest of the tale is improper.

❋

There once was a maiden Circassian
Who was loved by a courtier of fashion.
    When he vowed he adored her,
    * * * * * * * * * * * * * * *
(The asterisks indicate passion.)

❋

There was a young lady of Slough
Who said that she didn't know hough.
   Then a young fellow caught her
   And jolly well taught her:
And she can't have enough of it nough.

❋

There was a young lady from Hadham
Very fond of the primitive Adam.
   Whatever the name
   Of the men on the game,
The madam from Hadham had had 'em.

❋

There was a young fellow named Skinner,
Who once took a girl out to dinner.
  At a quarter to nine,
  They sat down to dine;
At a quarter past ten it was in her.
(The dinner, not Skinner.
Skinner was in her before dinner.)

Historical, Classical
&
Biblical

Now what in the world shall we dioux
With the bloody and murderous Sioux,
  Who some time ago
  Took an arrow and bow
And raised such a hellabelioux?

✳

There once was a damsel named Jinx,
Who when asked what she thought of the Sphinx,
  Replied with a smile,
  'That old fraud by the Nile?
I personally think that she stinks.'

✳

The conquering Lion of Judah
Made a prayer to the statue of Buddha.
  'O Idol,' he prayed,
  'May Il Duce be spayed,
And all his descendants be neuter!'

✳

Have you heard about Madame Lupescu,
Who came to Rumania's rescue?
  It's a wonderful thing
  To be under a king.
Is democracy better? I ask you!

✳

Royal Spasm in Five Fits

Thus spake the King of Siam:
'For women I don't care a damn;
    But a fat-bottomed boy
    Is my pride and my joy –
They call me a bugger: I am.'

✳

'Indeed,' quoth the King of Siam,
'For cunts I just don't give a damn.
    They haven't the grip,
    Nor the velvety tip,
Nor the scope of the asshole of man.'

✳

Then up spake the Bey of Algiers
And said to his harem, 'My dears,
    You may think it odd 'f me
    But I've given up sodomy –
Tonight there'll be fucking!' (*Loud cheers*)

✳

Then up spake the young King of Spain:
'To fuck and to bugger is pain.
    But it's not *infra dig*
    On occasion to frig,
And I do it again and again.'

✳

Then up spake a Hindu mahout,
And said, 'What's all this blithering about?
    Why, I shoot my spunk
    Up an elephant's trunk – '
(*Cries of* 'Shame! He's a shit! Throw him out!')

✳

I, Caesar, when I learned of the fame
Of Cleopatra, I straightway laid claim.
 Ahead of my legions,
 I invaded her regions –
I saw, I conquered, I came.

✳

There was a sweet lassie named Harriet
Who would take on two lads in a chariot;
 Then six monks and four tailors,
 Nine priests and eight sailors,
Pontius Pilate and Judas Iscariot.

✳

Brigham Young was never a neutah,
A pansy or fairy or fruitah.
 Where ten thousand virgins
 Succumbed to his urgin's
We now have the great state of Utah.

✳

There once was a Hun, named Attila,
Whose life was a genuine thrilla.
 From village to village
 He'd rant, rape and pillage,
Seldom spending two nights on one pilla.

✳

His neighbours objected, it's true,
To the way he would plunder and screw.
　　But he'd say, ' 'Tain't my fault,
　　'Cause it's all the reasult
Of a trauma I suffered at two.'

✳

When Cupid loved Psyche, it seems
That their sex-life was one of extremes.
　　Their performance in bed
　　Exceeded, it's said,
The wildest sex orgies of dreams.

✳

　Said Queen Isabella of Spain,
　'I like it now and again –
　　　But I wish to explain
　　　That by "now and again"
　I mean now and again and again.'

✳

Cleopatra, when sex was still new to her,
Kept buying up young slaves to tutor her.
　　But the Pharaoh (her dad)
　　For fear she'd go bad
Kept rendering them neuterer and neuterer.

✳

There was a young monarch called Ed
Who took Mrs Simpson to bed!
    As they bounced up and down,
    He said, 'Bugger the Crown!
We'll give it to Bertie instead.'

✳

If you're speaking of actions immoral,
Then how about giving the laurel
    To doughty Queen Esther?
    No three men could best her –
One fore and one aft and one oral.

✳

Old Louis Quatorze was hot stuff.
He tired of that game, blind man's buff;
    Upended his mistress,
    Kissed hers, while she kissed his,
And thus taught the world *soixante-neuf*.

✳

An elderly harlot from Trings
Has fucked the last four Spanish kings.
    Says she, 'They're all short
    And no good at the sport;
But the queen, who is Lesbian, swings.'

❋

Salome! Salome! Where art?
Thou biblical strip-teasing tart!
   I'd have thought that instead
   Of Jokanaan's head,
Thou'd'st have asked a more pertinent part.

❋

There've been many illustrious whores –
Salomes, Nell Gwynnes, Pompadours –
 But none so notorious,
 So lovely and glorious
As the mistress of Louis Quatorze.

❋

When Oedipus entered, erect,
Jocasta screamed, 'Stop! I object.
 You're a Greek! Screw some other –
 A goat, or your brother –
Mother-fucking's a little suspect.'

❋

In the Garden of Eden lay Adam,
Complacently stroking his madam,
 And great was his mirth,
 For he knew that on earth
There were only two balls – and he had 'em.

❋

In the speech of his time did the Bard
Refer to his prick as his 'yard';
 But sigh no more, madams,
 'Twas no longer than Adam's
Or mine – and not one half so hard!

✳

Queen Mary found Scotsmen are built
With a truly remarkable tilt:
   To her royal surprise
   Every member would rise
Each time she reached under a kilt.

✳

A palaeontologist, Locke,
Found a fossilised Jurassic cock.
   'Is it Tyrannosaurus?
   It's huge, black and porous –
And Christ, it's still hard as a rock!'

✳

An old archaeologist, Throstle,
Discovered a marvellous fossil.
   He could tell from its bend
   And the knob on the end
'Twas the peter of Paul the Apostle.

✳

As Apollo was chasing the fair
Daphne, she vanished in air.
   He could find but a shrub
   With thick bark on the hub
And not even a knot-hole to spare.

❋

When Lazarus came back from the dead
He still couldn't function in bed.
   'What good's resurrection
   Without an erection?'
Old Lazarus testily said.

❋

Consider the Emperor Nero –
Of many lewd tales he's the hero –
   Though he scraped on the fiddle,
   He just couldn't diddle –
And his *real* batting average was zero.

❋

In bed, the Romantics were vile
(Lord Byron apart). Shelley's style
   Was to lick his wife's belly,
   While poor Mary Shelley
Wrote *Frankenstein*, grimly, meanwhile.

❋

The Shah of the Empire of Persia
Lay for days in a sexual merger.
   When the nautch asked the Shah,
   'Won't you ever withdraw?'
He replied, 'It's not love; it's inertia.'

✳

There was a young lady named Gloria
Who was had by Sir Gerald du Maurier,
  And then by six men,
  Sir Gerald again,
And the band at the Waldorf-Astoria.

✳

Said the boy king: 'I fear I've a funny
Feeling down here in my tummy.'
  'Tut, tut!' said old Ra,
  'I can see that you are
Not a son, nor a dad, but a mummy.'

❋

Of the Georges, it's thought that the Ist
Although bad was by no means the worst.
   The IIIrd one is reckoned
   Much worse than the IInd,
And the IInd much worse than the Ist.

❋

A queen of old Egypt named Cleo
Conducted her loving 'con brio'.
   She felt quite at home in
   The arms of one Roman
But preferred to be part of a trio.

❋

Said Oedipus Rex, growing red,
'Those head-shrinkers! Would they were dead!
   They make such a pother
   Because I love mother –
Well, should I love father instead?'

❋

An Olympian lecher was Zeus,
Always playing around fast and loose,
   With one hand in the bodice
   Of some likely young goddess
And the other preparing to goose.

Homosexual,
Deviational
& Aberrational

The Grecians were famed for fine art
And buildings and stonework so smart.
   They distinguished with poise
   The men from the boys
And used crowbars to keep them apart.

✳

'I would doubt,' said the Bishop of Balham,
'Whether Tennyson ever screwed Hallam.
   Such things are best hid.
   Let us hope that he did:
De mortuis nil nisi malum.'

✳

There was a young fellow named Keyte
Who minced as he walked down the street.
   He wore shoes of bright red
   And playfully said,
'I may not be thtrong, but I'm thweet.'

✳

An astronomer, pious but odd
(To be honest, a dirty old sod),
   Who'd searched for a sign
   Of the presence divine,
Cried, 'I've just found Uranus, dear God!'

221

✳

A glutted debauchee from Frome
Lured beauteous boys to his home,
   Whereupon he would strip them
   And generally whip them
With rods of fine birch or of broom.

✳

There was a young pansy named Gene
Who cruised a sadistic Marine.
   Said the man with a smirk
   As they got down to work,
'In this game the Jack beats the Queen.'

✳

There was a Scots boy scout from Airdrie
Whose bottom was always kept bared. He
   Explained, 'The scout master
   Can enter me faster,
And a boy scout must aye be prepared. See?'

✳

As he lay in his bath mused Lord Byng,
'O Vimy! What memories you bring:
   That gorgeous young trooper . . .
   Er . . . No! . . . Gladys Cooper!
By Gad, sir! That was a near thing!'

✳

A pansy who lived in Khartoum
Took a lesbian up to his room,
   And they argued a lot
   About who should do what,
And how, and with which, and to whom.

✳

   Said a lesbian lady, 'It's sad;
   Of all of the girls that I've had,
     None gave me the thrill
     Of real rapture, until
I learned how to be a tribade.'

✳

That naughty old Sappho of Greece
Said, 'What I prefer to a piece,
   Is to have my pudenda
   Rubbed hard by the end o'
The little pink nose of my niece.'

✳

There was a young sailor named Xavier
Who cared not for God, nor his Saviour.
   He walked on the decks
   Displaying his sex
And was brigged for indecent behaviour

✳

A neurotic young playboy named Gleason
Liked boys for no tangible reason.
   A frontal lobotomy
   Cured him of sodomy
But ruined his plans for the season.

✳

There was a young Fellow of Wadham
Who asked for a ticket to Sodom.
   When they said, 'We prefer
   Not to issue them, sir,'
He said, 'Don't call me sir! Call me modom.'

✳

Said a former Prince Edward of Wales:
'I know now what marriage entails,
   So I don't want a girl
   But a jolly young earl,
To solace my passion for males.'

✳

There once was a Warden of Wadham
Who approved of the folkways of Sodom.
   'For a man might,' he said,
   'Have a very poor head
But be a fine fellow, at bottom.'

✳

Our ship's captain, nicknamed Old Randy,
Makes advances to any girl handy;
 But when shipwrecked a while
 On a bleak desert isle,
He made do with midshipman Sandy.

✳

There was once an effeminate Ottoman;
For the fair sex, I fear, he was not a man.
   He was all up in arms
   Against feminine charms:
'Quite frankly,' he said, 'I'm a bottom man.'

✳

There was an old bugger of Como
Who suddenly cried: 'Ecce Homo!'
   He tracked his man down
   To the heart of the town,
And gobbled him off in the duomo.

✳

A convict once, out in Australia,
Said unto his turnkey, 'I'll tail yer.'
   But he said, 'You be buggered,
   You filthy old sluggard,
You're forgetting as I am your gaoler.'

✳

There was an old Warden of Wadham, he
Was very much given to sodomy,
   But he shyly confessed,
   'I like tongue-fucking best,
God bless my soul, isn't it odd of me?'

There was a young person called Herman
Who spoke both falsetto and German.
  Behind the blond hair
  There was somebody there
But its sex one could never determine.

If Leo your own birthday marks
You will lust until forty, when starts
  A new pleasure in stamps,
  Boy scouts and their camps,
And fondling nude statues in parks.

❊

A tourist in Rome, from South Bend,
Decried sodomy to an old friend.
    Leered a visiting Bulgar:
    'You may say it's vulgar,
But you will find it's fun, in the end.'

❊

A prince with a temper outrageous
Had a palace replete with young pages.
    They were used for skulduggery
    And much royal buggery,
And he castrated some in his rages.

❊

A remarkable race are the Persians
They have such peculiar diversions.
    They make love all day
    In the regular way,
And save up the night for perversions.

❊

It seems that all our perversions
Were known to the Medes and the Persians.
    But the French and the Yanks
    Earn our undying thanks
For inventing some modernised versions.

✳

A sodomist, fresh out of gaol,
Was desperate for some sort of tail.
   By necessity forced
   He screwed the exhaust
Of a van clearly marked 'Royal Mail'.

✳

On the talk show last night Dr Ellis
(The sex shrink) took two hours to tell us,
   'It's all right to enjoy
   A rosy-cheeked boy –
So long as your sheep don't get jealous.'

✳

Said a co-ed from Duke University,
When asked about sexual perversity,
   'I find it's OK
   In the old-fashioned way,
But I do like a touch of diversity.'

❋

There was a young Turkish cadet –
And this is the damnedest one yet –
   His tool was so long
   And incredibly strong
He could bugger six Greeks *en brochette*.

❋

There was a young fellow called Chubb
Who joined a smart buggery club;
   But his parts were so small,
   He was no use at all,
And they promptly refunded his sub.

❋

Said an unhappy female named Sears,
'The world seems just full of those queers!
   At parties I go to
   Are no men to say no to;
They swish about, waggling their rears.'

❋

There was a young fellow, McBride,
Who preferred his trade long, thick and wide;
   But he never rejected
   Whatever erected,
For, 'Peter is peter,' he sighed.

Matrimonial,
Connubial &
Uxorial

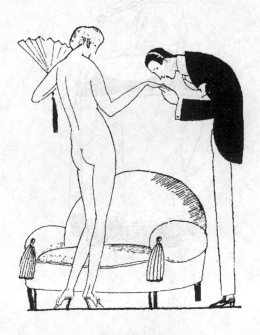

In Boston a sub-deb named Brooks
Had a hobby of reading sex books.
    She married a Cabot
    Who looked like a rabbit
And deftly lived up to his looks.

✳

There was an old widower, Doyle,
Who wrapped up his wife in tin foil.
    He thought it would please her
    To stay in the freezer
And anyway, outside she'd spoil.

✳

A dentist who lives in Duluth
Has wedded a widow named Ruth.
    She is so sentimental
    Concerning things dental,
She calls her dear second her 'twoth'.

✳

There was a young lady of Harwich
Whose conduct was odd at her marwich.
    She proceeded on skates
    To the parish church gates
While her friends followed on in a carwich.

✳

A sultan, inspecting his harem,
Said, 'Eunuch, proceed to lay bare 'em.'
    Having seen the details
    He issued long veils
And ordered the harem to wear 'em.

✳

To his wife said Sir Hubert de Dawes:
'Fix this chastity belt round your drawers!'
    But an amorous Celt
    Found the key to the belt
While the Squire was away at the wars.

✳

There was a young fellow of Beaulieu,
Who loved a fair maiden most treaulieu.
    He said, 'Do be mine,'
    And she didn't decline;
So the wedding was solemnised deaulieu.

✳

A young Englishwoman named St John
Met a red-skinned American It John
    Who made her his bride
    And gave her, beside,
A dress with a gaudy bead Frt John.

❋

A certain young chap named Bill Beebee
Was in love with a lady named Phoebe;
  'But,' he said, 'I must see
  What the clerical fee
Be before Phoebe be Phoebe Beebee.'

❋

There was a young bride named McWing
Who thought sex a delirious fling.
  When her bridegroom grew ill
  From too much (as they will),
She found other men do the same thing.

❋

A certain old maid in Cohoes
In despair taught her bird to propose;
  But the parrot, dejected
  At being accepted,
Spoke some lines too profane to disclose.

❋

There was a young lady of Harwich
Who said on the morn of her marriage,
  'I shall sew my chemise
  Right down to my knees,
For I'm damned if I fuck in the carriage!'

235

❋

When Carol was told about sex,
She said, 'Mother, it sounds so complex.
   Do you mean you and father
   Went through all that bother,
And I'm just the after-effects?'

❋

An innocent bride from the mission
Remarked, on her first night's coition:
   'What an intimate section
   To use for connection –
And, Lord! what a silly position!'

❋

A delighted, incredulous bride
Remarked to the groom at her side,
   'I never could quite
   Believe till tonight
Our anatomies would coincide!'

❋

Said the newlyweds staying near Whiteley,
'We turn out the electric light nightly.
   It's best to embark
   Upon sex in the dark;
The look of the thing's so unsightly.'

✳

A young bride and groom of Australia
Remarked as they joined genitalia:
  'Though the system seems odd,
  We are thankful that God
Developed the genus Mammalia.'

✳

On a date with a charming young bird
His erotic emotions were stirred.
  So with bold virile pluck,
  He enquired, 'Do you fuck?'
She said, 'Yes, but please don't use that word.'

❋

The wife of an absent dragoon
Begged a soldier to grant her a boon:
   As she let down her drawers,
   She said, 'It's all yours –
I could deal with the whole damned platoon!'

❋

There's an over-sexed lady named White
Who insists on a dozen a night.
   A fellow named Cheddar
   Had the brashness to wed her –
His chance of survival is slight.

❋

To a whore, said the cold Lady Dizzit,
'Lord D's a new man, since your visit.
   As a rule, the damned fool
   Can't erect his old tool.
You must have what it takes; but what is it?'

❋

I did feel obliged to friend Fife
For the overnight use of his wife.
   But he dropped in today
   And insisted on pay –
Such sordidness sours me on life.

✳

There once was a *maître d'hôtel*,
Who said, 'They can all go to hell!
  They make love to my wife
  And it ruins my life,
For the worst is, they do it so well!'

✳

There was a young lady of Eton
Whose figure had plenty of meat on.
  She said, 'Marry me, dear,
  And you'll find that my rear
Is a nice place to warm your cold feet on.'

❋

A near-sighted fellow named Walter,
Led a glamorised lass to the altar;
　　A beauty he thought her,
　　Till some soap and water
Made her look like the Rock of Gibraltar.

❋

There was a young fellow named Hammer
Who had an unfortunate stammer.
　　'The b–bane of my life,'
　　He said, 'is m–my wife.
D–d–d–d–d–d–damn her.'

❋

A young trapeze artist named Bract
Is faced by a very sad fact:
　　Imagine his pain,
　　When, again and again,
He catches his wife in the act!

❋

There was a young fellow named Keating
Whose pride took a terrible beating.
　　That happens to males
　　When they learn the details
Of their wives' extra-marital cheating.

❋

An eager young bride, Mrs Strong,
Thought that passion would last all night long,
   And her husband's capacity
   Would match her voracity –
But (alas!) it transpired she was wrong.

❋

An astonished young bride in Hong Kong
Found her husband abnormally strong.
   She knew about sex
   And its heady effects,
But thought thirty-two times might be wrong.

❋

There was an old fellow of Lyme
Who lived with three wives at a time.
   When asked, 'Why the third?'
   He replied, 'One's absurd;
And bigamy, sir, is a crime.'

❋

There was a young lady of Pinner
Whose hubby came home to his dinner;
   And guess what he saw
   As he opened the door?
The butt of the man who was in her,

✳

A widow who lived in Rangoon
Hung a black-ribboned wreath o'er her womb,
 'To remind me,' she said,
 'Of my husband, who's dead;
And of what put him into his tomb.'

✳

There was a gay Countess of Dufferin,
 One night while her husband was covering,
  Just to chaff him a bit,
  She said, 'You old shit,
 I can buy a dildo for a sovereign.'

✳

At his wedding a bridegroom named Crusoe
Was embarrassed to find his prick grew so.
 His eager young bride
 Pulled him quickly astride
And was screwed while still wearing her trousseau.

✳

A hot-tempered girl of Caracas
 Was wed to a samba-mad jackass;
  When he started to cheat her
  With a dark senorita,
 She kicked him right in the maracas.

Sighed a newlywed damsel of Wheeling,
'A honeymoon sounds so appealing,
　　But for nearly two weeks
　　I've heard only bed squeaks
And seen nothing but cracks in the ceiling.'

　　An octogenarian Jew
　　To his wife remained steadfastly true.
　　　　This was not from compunction,
　　　　But due to dysfunction
　　Of his spermatic glands – nuts to you.

✳

There was a young parson of Harwich
Tried to grind his betrothed in a carriage.
   She said, 'No, you young goose,
    Just try self-abuse,
And the other we'll try after marriage.'

✳

There was an old person of Goshem
Who took out his bollocks to wash 'em.
   His wife said, 'Now, Jack,
    If you don't put them back,
I'll step on the buggers and squash 'em.'

✳

A suspicious old husband from Funtua
To his wife said, 'How bulky in front you are.
   You have not been imprudent,
    I hope, with some student?'
She replied, 'Really, dear, how blunt you are!'

✳

A newlywed husband named Lyneham
Asked his bride if she'd first 'sixty-nine' him.
   When she just shook her head,
    He sighed and then said,
'Well, if we can't lick 'em, let's jine 'em.'

✳

When the judge with his wife having sport,
Proved suddenly two inches short,
   The good lady declined,
    And the judge had her fined
By proving contempt of his court.

✳

A mortician who practised in Fife
Made love to the corpse of his wife.
   'How could I know, judge?
    She was cold and did not budge –
Just the same as she'd been all her life.'

✳

A remarkable fellow named Clarence
Had learned self-control from his parents;
   With his wife in the nude
    He'd just sit there and brood,
And practise the art of forbearance.

✳

There once was a matron of Ottawa
Whose husband, she said, thought a lot of her;
   Which, to give him his due
    Was probably true,
Since he'd sired twenty kids, all begot on her.

✳

There was a young farmer named Morse
Who fell madly in love with his horse.
  Said his wife, 'You rapscallion,
  That horse is a stallion –
This constitutes grounds for divorce.'

✳

In summer he said she was fair,
In autumn her charms were still there:
  But he said to his wife,
  In the winter of life,
'There's no spring in your old *derrière*.'

✳

A newlywed couple from Goshen
Spent their honeymoon sailing the ocean.
  In twenty-eight days
  They got laid eighty ways:
Imagine such fucking devotion!

✳

A lady was once heard to weep,
'My figure no more I can keep.
  It's my husband's demand
  For a tit in each hand,
And the bastard will walk in his sleep!'

✳

There once was a sensitive bride
Who ran when the groom she espied.
    When she looked at his swiver
    They had to revive her,
But when he got it well in, she just sighed.

✳

    Lady Reginald Humphries (belie-
    Ve it or not) had a vulva so wee
        She disposed of the sexual
        Needs of Lord Rex through a l-
    Audably disciplined flea.

✳

A certain young bride from Key West
Was uncommonly large in the chest.
    Her man's close attention
    To her outsize dimension
Brought his own measurement to its best.

✳

There was a young man of Cape Cod
Who once put my wife into pod.
    His name it was Tucker
    The dirty old fucker,
The bugger, the blighter, the sod!

248

✳

There once was a woman of Churston
Who thought her third husband the worst 'un –
    For he justly was reckoned
    Far worse than the second,
And her second was worse than the first 'un.

✳

There once was a fellow named Simon
Who for years couldn't pierce his wife's hymen,
    Till he hit on the trick
    Of sheathing his prick
In a steel condom tipped with a diamond.

✳

She wore knickers of delicate mauve
And her temper was fiendish, or fauve;
   She had a nineteen-inch waist,
   And she married (in haste)
The Town Clerk of Brighton and Hove.

✳

There was an old fellow from Fife
Who was garden mad all of his life.
   He dreamt in his slumbers
   Of giant cucumbers –
Which greatly embarrassed his wife.

✳

There was a young lady named Kent,
Who gave up her husband for Lent.
   The night before Easter,
   When Jesus released her,
It didn't make a damned bit of difference
because in the meantime he'd been
running around with a whole lot of other
women.

Medical,
Psychological
& Problematical

Tom's sister, called Lucy O'Finner,
Grew constantly thinner and thinner;
   The reason was plain –
   She slept out in the rain,
And was never allowed any dinner.

✳

There once was a man of Calcutta
Who spoke with a terrible stutter;
   At breakfast he said,
   'Give me some b–bread
And b–b–b–b–b–b–butter.'

✳

There once were some learned MDs
Who captured some germs of disease
   And infected a train,
   Which, without causing pain,
Allowed one to catch it with ease.

✳

There was a young farmer from Slough
Who said, 'I've a terrible cough.
   Do you think I should get
   Both the doc and the vet,
Or would one be enough for now?'

✳

Whenever he got in a fury, a
Schizophrenic from Upper Manchuria
Had pseudocyesis,
Disdiadochokinesis
And haemotoporphyrimuria.

✳

There was a young man who said, 'Damn!
At last I've found out that I am
A creature that moves
In determinate grooves:
In fact, not a bus but a tram.'

✳

An eccentric old lady of Honiton
(Whose conduct I once wrote a sonnet on)
Has now been in bed
With a cold in her head,
For a week, with her boots and her bonnet on.

✳

There was a fair maiden of Warwick
Who lived in the castle histarwick.
On the damp castle mould
She contracted a could,
And the doctor prescribed paregarwick.

✳

An unpopular man of Cologne
With a pain in his stomach did mogne;
He heaved a great sigh,
And said: 'I would digh,
But the loss would be simply my ogne.'

✳

Once a charming young lass from Listowel,
Whose beauty was everyone's goal,
   In her efforts to please
   Spread a well-known disease
From Slea Head to the frosty South Pole.

✳

There was a young girl from Samoa
Who said to a sailor named Noah,
   'You can kiss me and squeeze me,
   But remember, to please me,
I'm allergic to spermatozoa.'

✳

She wasn't what one would call pretty
And other girls offered her pity;
   So nobody guessed
   That her Wasserman test
Involved half the men in the city

＊

To his nurse said the famous physician,
In the throes of illicit coition:
    'Though it's getting quite late,
    Let the damn patients wait!
Please assume the *post-partum* position.'

＊

The enjoyment of sex, although great,
Is in later years said to abate.
    This well may be so,
    I'm afraid I don't know,
For I'm now only seventy-eight.

＊

According to old Sigmund Freud,
Life is seldom so well enjoyed
    As in human coition
    (In any position)
With the usual organs employed.

＊

A lissom psychotic named Jane
Once kissed every man on a train.
    Said she, 'Please don't panic,
    I'm just nymphomanic –
It wouldn't be fun, were I sane.'

❋

A young man whose sight was myopic
Thought sex an incredible topic.
    So poor were his eyes
    That despite its great size
His penis appeared microscopic.

❋

An unfortunate lad from Madrid
Had both Super-Ego and Id,
    So whether he screwed
    Or completely eschewed
He felt guilty, whatever he did.

❋

A lad, grown too tight, one supposes,
Was dreadfully sore with phimosis.
    The doctor said, 'Why,
    Circumcision we'll try –
A plan recommended by Moses.'

❋

A mosquito was heard to complain
That a chemist had poisoned his brain;
    The cause of his sorrow
    Was Paradichloro-
Diphenyltrichlorothane.

✳

A psychiatrist said, 'It's no matter
That my husband is mad as a hatter.
    There are certain psychoses
    That bring sex in large doses –
My husband, you see, is a satyr.'

✳

A sex-mad young gay boy named Willie
Whose antics are frequently silly,
    Has had, just for fun,
    A vasectomy done –
An instance of 'gelding the lily'.

✳

In Utrecht the great Dr Strabismus
Found his bride had acute vaginismus;
    His very first fuck,
    He found himself stuck,
And had to stay in her till Christmas.

✳

There was a young fellow of Burma
Whose betrothed had good reason to murmur;
    But now that he's married he's
    Using cantharides
And the root of their love is much firmer

✳

There was a young lady of Chiswick,
Who consulted a doctor of physic;
    He tested her hormones,
    And sexual performones,
Then prescribed her a strong aphrodisic.

✳

Artificial insemination
Some say will replace fornication;
    But perish the day
    When the old-fashioned way
Can't supply enough kids for the nation!

✳

There was a young lady of Michigan
Who said, 'Damn it! I've got the itch again.'
    Said her mother, 'That's strange,
    I'm surprised it ain't mange,
If you've slept with that son-of-a-bitch again.'

✳

Though the practice of young Heloise is
To pleasure whomever she pleases,
    She admits the one hitch is
    She suffers from itches
And various social diseases.

❋

There was a young fellow named Pfister
Who noticed an odd sort of blister
   Where no blister should be;
   What was worse, do you see,
He had got it at home from his sister.

❋

There was a young bounder named Fisk
Whose method of screwing was brisk;
   And his reason was: 'If
   The damned bitch has the syph,
This way I'm reducing the risk.'

❋

There was a young girl from Mauritius
Who said, 'That last bout was delicious.
   But if you don't mind,
   We'll postpone the next grind,
As that spot on your tool looks suspicious.'

❋

There was a young woman of Chester
Who said to the man who undressed her,
   'I think you will find
   That it's better behind –
The front is beginning to fester.'

✳

There was a young woman of Cheadle
Who once gave the clap to a beadle.
　　Said she, 'Does it itch?'
　　'It does, you damned bitch,
And burns like hell-fire when I peedle.'

✳

There was a young lady named Hitchin
Who was scratching her crotch in the kitchen.
　　Her mother said, 'Rose,
　　It's the crabs, I suppose.'
She said, 'Yes, and the buggers are itchin'.'

✳

There was a young lady at sea
Who complained that it hurt her to pee.
　　'Indeed?' said the mate.
　　'That accounts for the state
Of the captain, the purser and me.'

✳

Said the Earl to the Countess of Cottam
(Who had crabs, but knew not where'd got 'em):
　　'My dear, you're too generous
　　With your *mons Veneris*
And equally so with your bottom.'

*

There was a young girl of Bavaria
Who thought her disease was malaria,
    But the family doc
    Explained to her shock,
'It began in your genital area.'

*

A worried teenager from Poole
Discovered red spots on his tool.
    Said the doctor, a cynic,
    'Get out of my clinic –
Just wipe off the lipstick, you fool!'

*

There once was a doughty Norwegian
Who enlivened the French Foreign Legion;
    But his brothers-in-arms
    Who succumbed to his charms
Got the clap in their hindermost region.

*

There was a young girl of Uttoxeter,
And all the young men shook their cocks at her.
    From one of these cocks
    She contracted the pox,
And she poxed all the cocks in Uttoxeter.

✳

The spouse of a pretty young thing,
Came home from the wars in the spring.
　　He was lame but he came
　　With his dame like a flame –
A discharge is a wonderful thing.

✳

There was a young girl of high station
Who ruined her fine reputation
　　When she said she'd the pox
　　From sucking on cocks –
She should really have called it 'fellation'.

✳

A girl to the druggist did say,
'I am bothered with bugs in my hay.'
　　'I see what you mean –
　　You need Paris green
To be rid of the things right away.'

✳

The results of this piece of mischance
Were disastrous, you'll see at a glance.
　　First died bugs, then went trees,
　　Then her pet Pekinese,
And two gentlemen just in from France.

264

✳

Said a butcher's apprentice from Frome
Who aspired to be bride (and not groom),
  'With some knives from the shop,
    I shall do my own op' –
And these words are inscribed on his tomb.

✳

There was once an eccentric old boffin
Who remarked, in a fine fit of coughing,
  'It isn't the cough
    That carries you off,
But the coffin they carry you off in.'

✳

There was an old fellow named Hewing,
Whose heart stopped while he was a-screwing;
  He gasped: 'Really, miss,
    Don't feel bad about this –
There's nothing I'd rather die doing.'

✳

If intercourse gives you thrombosis,
And continence causes neurosis,
  I'd rather expire
    Fulfilling desire
Than live in a state of psychosis.

✳

There was a young man from Laconia,
Whose mother-in-law had pneumonia.
    He hoped for the worst
    And after March 1st
They buried her 'neath a begonia.

✳

A young schizophrenic named Struther,
When told of the death of his brother,
    Said: 'Yes, it's too bad,
    But I can't feel too sad –
After all, I still have each other.'

✳

There was a faith-healer of Deal
Who said: 'Although pain isn't real,
    If I sit on a pin,
    And it punctures my skin,
I dislike what I fancy I feel.'

✳

The girls who frequent picture palaces
Set no store by psychoanalysis.
    Indeed, they're annoyed
    By the great Dr Freud,
And they cling to their long-standing fallacies.

✳

Job's comforters now are emphatic
That his illnesses – whether rheumatic,
 Sclerotic, arthritic,
 Myopic, paralytic –
Were, quite simply, psychosomatic.

✳

The masses, declaimed Dr Freud,
Are seldom so peacefully employed
 As in the position
 Described as coition,
So it's nice that it's widely enjoyed.

✳

There was an old man of Belfast
Whose active sex life was so vast;
    He'd blithely worked through
    To a spry ninety-two
But his lust was declining at last.

✳

A girl being treated for hernia
Remarked to her doctor, Goldernia,
    'When slicing my middle
    Be sure not to fiddle
With matters that do not concernya.'

✳

There was an old man of the Isles
Who suffered severely from pisles.
    He couldn't sit down
    Without a deep frown,
So he had to row standing for misles.

✳

There was a young man from Toledo
Who travelled about incognito.
    The reason he did
    Was to bolster his id
Whilst appeasing his savage libido.

Musical,
Theatrical
& Acrobatical

There was a young lady of Norway
Who hung by her toes in a doorway.
    She said to her beau:
    'Just look at me, Joe,
I think I've discovered one more way.'

✱

Some amateur players, most brave,
A performance of *Hamlet* once gave.
    Said a wag, 'Now let's see
    If it's Bacon or he –
I mean Shakespeare – who's turned in his grave.'

✱

There was an old lady of Tooting
Who wanted to learn parachuting.
    Though they tried to repress her,
    She jumped from the dresser,
A perfect vol-plane executing.

✱

A tone-deaf old fellow of Tring,
When somebody asked him to sing,
    Replied, 'It is odd,
    But I cannot tell "God
Save the Weasel" from "Pop goes the King".'

✳

A singer in Radio City
(Whose form is impressively pretty)
   Is often addressed
   By the name of 'Beau Chest',
Which is thought to be tasteful and witty.

✳

There was a young man of Hong Kong
Who invented a topical song.
   It wasn't the words
   That bothered the birds
But the horrible double ontong.

✳

There were three little owls in a wood
Who sang hymns whenever they could.
   What the words were about
   One could never make out,
But one felt it was doing them good.

✳

There was a young lady of Ealing
Who had an irrational feeling
   That she was a fly
   And she felt she should try
To walk upside down on the ceiling.

✳

There once was a corpulent carp
Who wanted to play on the harp;
   But to his chagrin,
   So short was his fin,
He couldn't reach up to C sharp.

✳

Elgar's opera *At the Boar's Head*
As a title makes no one's face red –
   Save Jessica Hood's
   (Most prudish of prudes),
Who thinks of what Spooner'd have said!

*

There was a composer named Liszt
Whose music no one could resiszt.
    When he swept the keyboard
    Nobody could be bored,
And now that he's gone he is miszt.

*

Of a sudden, the great prima donna
Cried: 'Gawd: my voice is a gonner.'
    But a cat in the wings
    Said: 'I know how she sings,'
And finished the solo with honour.

*

There was a young lady named Hatch
Who doted on music by Bach.
    She played with her pussy
    To *The Faun* by Debussy,
But to ragtime she just scratched her snatch.

*

A *musicienne* in gay Montebello
Amused herself playing the cello,
    But not a solo,
    For she used as a bow
The dong of a sturdy young fellow.

❋

A baritone star of Havana
Slipped horribly on a banana;
    He was sick for a year
    Then resumed his career –
As a promising lyric soprano.

❋

We've got a new maid called Chrysanthemum
Who said, 'I have just come from Grantham, m'm.
    I lost my last place
    In the sorest disgrace,
'Cos I snored through the National Anthem, m'm.'

❋

'My girlfriend wants me to ski,'
Said the flabby young cellist, 'but gee!
    With Stravinsky, Stokowski,
    Mussorgsky, Tchaikovsky,
That's quite enough skiing for me.'

❋

A famous theatrical actress
Played best in the role of malefactress;
    Yet her home life was pure
    Except, to be sure,
A scandal or two just for practice.

❋

A certain young sheik I'm not namin'
Asked an actress he thought he was tamin',
    'Have you your maidenhead?'
    'Don't be silly!' she said,
'But I still have the box that it came in.'

❋

The last time I dined with the king
He did a quite curious thing:
        He sat on a stool,
        And took out his tool,
And said, 'If I play, will you sing?'

❋

There was a young man from Madrid
Who discovered when only a kid
        That by lying supine
        And twisting his spine,
He could suck his own cock – so he did.

❋

There was a young lady of Brussels
Whose pride was her vaginal muscles;
        She could easily plex them
        And so interflex them
As to whistle love songs through her bustles.

✳

An organist playing at York
Had a prick that could hold a small fork,
    And between obbligatos
    He'd munch at tomatoes,
And keep up his strength while at work.

❋

There was a young fellow named Carse
Whose bollocks were fashioned from brass.
    When they tinkled together
    They played 'Stormy Weather'
And lightning shot out of his arse.

❋

There was a young dancer of Ipswich
Who took most astonishing skips, which
    So delighted a miss,
    She said, 'Give me a kiss!'
He replied, 'On the cheek, or the lips – which?'

❋

A concert conductor in Rio
Fell in love with a lady called Cleo;
    As she took down her panties,
    He said: 'No *andantes*!
I want it *allegro con brio*!'

❋

There was a young artist named Mentzel
Whose prick was as sharp as a pencil.
    He pierced through an actress,
    The sheet and the mattress,
And punctured the bedroom utensil.

✳

As Mozart composed a sonata
The maid bent to fasten her garter;
   Without any delay
   He started to play
Un poco piu appassionata.

✳

There once was a wicked old actor
Who waylaid a young girl and attacked her.
   In response to this trick
   She bit off his prick
And thus remained *virgo intacta.*

✳

There was a young fellow called Cager
Who, as the result of a wager,
   Offered to fart
   The whole oboe part
Of Mozart's *Quartet in F Major.*

✳

There was a young fellow from Sparta,
A really magnificent farter,
   On the strength of one bean
   He'd fart 'God Save the Queen'
And Beethoven's *Moonlight Sonata.*

✳

There was an old lady of Chislehurst
Who before she could pee had to whistle first.
  One day in late June,
  She forgot the right tune . . .
And sadly her over-stretched bladder burst!

✳

A pious old Jew from Salonika
Said, 'For Christmas I'd like a harmonica.'
  His wife, to annoy him,
  Said, 'Feh! That's for *goyim!*'
And gave him a jews-harp for Chanukah.

✳

There was a young girl in the choir
Whose voice rose hoir and hoir,
  Till it reached such a height
  It was clear out of seight –
And they found it next day on the spoir.

✳

A boy who played tunes on a comb,
Had become such a nuisance at homb,
  His ma spanked him, and then –
  'Will you do it again?'
And he cheerfully answered her, 'Nomb.'

*

There was a young lady of Bude
Who danced on the stage in the nude,
    When a fellow out front
    Stood up and said, 'Cunt,'
Just like that, right out loud, bloody rude!

*

The great violinist was bowing;
The quarrelsome oarsmen were rowing.
    But how is the sage
    To judge from the page:
Was it pigs or seeds that were sowing?

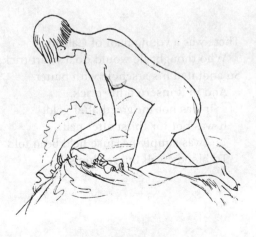

✳

The conductor, with voice like a hatchet,
Observed to a cellist from Datchet:
    'You have twixt your thighs,
    My dear, a great prize –
An instrument noted for beauty and size –
And yet you just sit there and scratch it!'

✳

A young violinist named Biddle
Played exceedingly well on the fiddle.
    Yet twixt women and art
    'Twas the girls won his heart
Hands down and hands up – and hands middle.

✳

There was a young man of Calcutta
    Who thought he would do a smart trick,
So anointed his arsehole with butter,
    And in it inserted his prick.
        It was not for greed after gold,
        It was not for thirst after pelf;
            'Twas simply because he'd been told
        To bloody well bugger himself.

Philosophical,
Academical
& Mathematical

There was an old person of Cromer
Who stood on one leg to read Homer;
    When he found he grew stiff,
    He jumped over the cliff,
Which concluded that person of Cromer.

✻

There once was a painter named Scott
Who seemed to have hair but had not.
    He seemed to have sense,
    'Twas an equal pretence
On the part of the painter named Scott.

✻

There was a young genius of Queen's
Who was fond of exploding machines.
    He once blew up a door,
    But he'll do it no more
For it chanced that the door was the Dean's.

✻

Said a logical linguist named Rolles,
'As we always call Polish folk Poles,
    For better precision
    (I am a logician)
We ought to call Dutch people Holes.'

*

There was a young poet of Kew
Who failed to emerge into view;
   So he said, 'I'll dispense
   With rhyme, metre and sense.'
And he did; and he's now in *Who's Who*.

*

There was an old man who said, 'Do
Tell me how I'm to add two and two.
   I'm not very sure
   That it doesn't make four,
But I fear that is almost too few.'

*

We've socially conscious biography,
Aesthetics and social geography;
   Today every field
   Boasts its Marxist yield,
So now we've class-conscious pornography.

*

There once was an artist named Lear
Who wrote verses to make children cheer.
   Though they never made sense
   Their success was immense
And the Queen thought that Lear was a dear.

✳

I'm bored to extinction with Harrison,
His limericks and puns are embarrassin'.
  But I'm fond of the bum
  For, though dull as they come,
He makes me feel bright by comparison.

✳

A foreigner said, 'I have heard
Your language is really absurd.
  The spelling is weird,
  Much worse than I feared,
For word rhymes with bird, nerd or turd.'

✳

There was a young poet of Trinity
Who, although he could trill like a
linnet, he
  Could never complete
  Any poem with feet,
Saying, 'Idiots,
Can't you see
That what I'm writing
Happens
To be
Free
Verse?'

❋

Ethnologists up with the Sioux
Wired home for 'two punts, one canoe'.
　　The answer next day
　　Said: 'Girls on the way,
But what in hell's name's a "panoe"?'

❋

There once was a fellow of Trinity
Who raised xyz to infinity;
　　And then the old brute
　　Extracted the root.
He afterwards took to Divinity.

❋

A right-handed writer named Wright
In writing 'write' always wrote 'rite',
　　When he meant to write 'write'.
　　If he'd written 'write' right,
Wright would not have wrought rot writing 'rite'.

❋

Said a boy to his teacher one day,
'Wright has not written "rite" right, I say.'
　　And the teacher replied,
　　As the error she eyed,
'Right! Wright: write "rite" right, right away!'

*

There was a young man of Japan,
Who wrote verses that never would scan.
   When folk told him so,
   He replied: 'Yes, I know,
But I always try and get as many words into
        the last line as I possibly can.'

*

There was a young man of Nepal
Who had a mathematical ball;
   The cube of its weight,
   Times pi, minus eight,
Is four thirds of the root of fuck all.

*

An assistant professor named Ddodd
Had manners arresting and odd.
   He said, 'If you please,
   Spell my name with four d's' –
Though one was sufficient for God.

*

A curious artist, Picasso:
His voice was remarkably basso,
   His balls were both cubic,
   His hair was all pubic.
Some thought him a bit of an arsehole.

❋

There's a wonderful family called Stein:
There's Gert and there's Ep and there's Ein.
   Gert's poems are bunk,
   Ep's statues are junk,
And no one can understand Ein.

❋

There was a young man of Cape Race,
Whose mind was an utter disgrace;
   He thought Marie Corelli
   Lived long before Shelley,
And that Wells was the name of a place.

❋

Ivy Compton-Burnett's irritations,
And the titles she gives her narrations . . .
   All these misses and misters,
   All those *Brothers and Sisters* –
They all sound like sexual relations.

❋

A limerick writer named Symes
Said, 'I'm so frustrated at times:
   I can do –ock and –uck,
   But with –unt I get stuck,
I'm really quite hopeless with rhymes.'

❊

There was an anthologist who
Decided that nought was taboo.
    Her words are so rude,
    Her verses so lewd,
I'm sure they'll appeal to you.

❊

An authoress, armed with a skewer,
Once hunted a hostile reviewer.
    'I'll teach him,' she cried,
    'When I've punctured his hide,
To call my last novel too pure.'

✳

A farmer from Ballymacoda,
Was awarded a special diploma
    For telling apart
    An animal fart
From a similar human aroma!

✳

A lonely old maid named Loretta
Sent herself an anonymous letter,
    Quoting Ellis on sex,
    And *Oedipus Rex*,
And exclaimed: 'I already feel better.'

✳

A complacent old don of Divinity
Made boast of his daughter's virginity.
    They must have been dawdlin'
    Down at old Magdalen –
It couldn't have happened at Trinity.

✳

While the prof wrote a Latin declension,
His pupils did things one can't mention,
    Like screwing and blowing
    Each other, and showing
A singular lack of attention.

✳

The cute little schoolteacher said,
As she gleefully hopped into bed:
   'If the lads and the lasses
   In my hygiene classes
Could see me right now, they'd drop dead!'

✳

An intelligent whore from Albania
Read books and grew steadily brainier.
   Yet it wasn't her science
   That brought her male clients
But her quite uncontrolled nymphomania.

✳

There was a young lady of parts,
Not one of your lower-class tarts;
   She had worked at St John's
   Under ten learned dons
And been certified Mistress of Arts.

✳

A Kentucky-bound author named Vaughan,
Whose style often savoured of scorn,
   Soon inscribed in his journals,
   'Here the corn's full of kernels,
And the colonels are all full of corn.'

❋

There was a young lawyer named Rex
Who was sadly deficient in sex.
  Arraigned for exposure,
  He said, with composure,
'*De minimis non curat lex.*'

❋

A tall rugger blue, up from Strood,
Strode along King's Parade in the nude.
  An old don said, 'What a m
  Agnificent bottom!'
And smacked it, as hard as he could!

❋

A philosopher known for sarcasm
Took a lass to his bed for orgasm,
  But found, to his shock,
  He had a limp cock,
And dismissed her as nothing but phantasm.

❋

There was a young lady of Brabant
Who slept with an impotent savant.
  She admitted, 'We shouldn't,
  But it turned out he couldn't;
So you can't say we have when we haven't!'

✳

Said an ape, as he swung by his tail,
To his offspring both female and male:
   'From *your* offspring, my dears,
   In a couple of years,
May evolve a professor at Yale.'

✳

Said Einstein, 'I have an equation
Which science might call Rabelaisian.
   Let P be virginity
   Approaching infinity
And U be a constant, persuasion.

❉

'Now, if P over U be inverted
And the square root of U be inserted
   X times over P,
   The result, QED,
Is a relative,' Einstein asserted.

❉

There was a young lady of Perth
Who said, 'Lord! I'm increasing in girth!'
   And her lovely young figure
   Grew steadily bigger
And bigger – till after the birth.

❉

Dr Johnson, when sober or pissed,
Could be frequently heard to insist,
   Letting out a great fart,
   'Yes, I follow Descartes –
I stink, and I therefore exist.'

❉

A maiden at college named Breeze,
Weighed down by BAs and Litt Ds,
   Collapsed from the strain.
   Alas, it was plain,
She was killing herself by degrees.

✳

There was a young man who said, 'Ayer
Has answered the atheist's prayer.
  For a hell one can't verify
  Surely can't terrify –
At least, till you know you are there.'

✳

An innocent lady in Cicester
One day asked an elderly visitor:
  'Now why's it illicit
  For a girl to solicit
When a man can become a solicitor?'

✳

There was a young student of John's
Who wanted to bugger the swans.
  But the loyal hall porter
  Said, 'Sir, take my daughter –
Those swans are reserved for the dons.'

✳

There once was a student of Trinity
Who ruined his sister's virginity;
  He buggered his brother,
  Had twins by his mother
And then took a degree in Divinity.

*

The career of a Fehllow called Castor
One day met with sudden disaster,
    When he came into Hall
    Wearing nothing at all
And made a rude sign at the Master.

*

There once was a Master of Jesus
Who one night slept with two of his nieces;
    To the first he gave twins,
    To the second one quins,
And, to both of them, frightful diseases.

*

A Classical Master of Arts
Told his wife he was still keen on tarts.
    Said she: 'That's just dandy,
    To think you're still randy:
You still know your principal parts.'

*

There was a young lady named Bright
Whose speed was far faster than light.
    She set off one day
    In a relative way
And came back the previous night.

✳

To her friends, that Miss Bright used to chatter:
'I have learned something new about matter:
    My speed was so great
    That it increased my weight
Yet I failed to become any fatter.'

✳

There was a strange fellow called Brecht
Whose penis was seldom erect.
    When his wife heard him humming
    She knew he was coming
On account of the Doppler effect.

✳

A scientist living at Staines
Is searching with infinite pains
　　For a new type of sound,
　　Which he hopes, when it's found,
Will travel much faster than planes.

✳

There was an old man of Nepal
Couldn't get Chomsky's wavelength at all:
　　While Teilhard du Chardin
　　Led him right up the jardin,
Levi-Strauss drove him straight up the wall.

✳

Two fishwives from neighbouring premises
Perpetually courted their nemesis.
　　They could never agree
　　In their quarrels, you see,
For they argued from different premises.

✳

There was a young student of Queen's
Who haunted the public latrines.
　　He was heard in the john
　　Saying, 'Bring me a don –
But spare me those dreary old Deans.'

✳

Said Shakespeare, 'I fear you're mistaken
If you think that my plays are by Bacon.
   I'm writing a book
   Proving Bacon's a crook
And his style's an obscure and opaque 'un.

✳

There was a young lady called Burton
Who outraged the Fellows of Girton
   By cycling to town
   Without wearing a gown
And, what's worse, without even a skirton.

✳

There once was a man who said, 'God
Must find it exceedingly odd
   If he finds that this tree
   Continues to be
When there's no one about in the Quad.'

✳

   Dear sir, Your astonishment's odd;
I am always about in the Quad;
     And that's why this tree
     Will continue to be
Since observed by Yours faithfully, God.

✳

A mathematician named Hall,
Has a hexahedronical ball,
   And the cube of its weight
   Times his pecker, plus eight,
Is his phone number – give him a call.

✳

An eccentric young poet named Brown
Raised up his embroiderèd gown
   To look for his peter,
   To beat it to metre,
But fainted when none could be found.

✳

A luscious young student at Vassar
Was hailed as a top-of-the-classer –
   But not in her studies,
   You old fuddy-duddies,
For she shone as a great piece-of-asser.

✳

A writer named Barbara Pym
Indulged in a personal whim:
   She'd wear a large bonnet
   When writing a sonnet
And a helmet when writing a hymn.

❋

There was a young poet of Thusis
Who went twilight walks with the
Muses;
　　But the nymphs of the air
　　Are not what they were
And the practice has led to abuses.

❋

There was a young fellow of Merton
Who went out with only his shirt on,
　　From which did peep shyly
　　His *membrum virile*,
For people to animadvert on.

❋

An astronomer fellow named Mark
Was sure it would be a great lark
　　To have a girl eye
　　The stars in the sky
And see what came up in the dark.

❋

A young teacher from far-off Bombay
Turned down a request for a lay,
　　Nicely couched in a note –
　　Since the fellow who wrote
Had spelled 'intercoarse' with an 'a'.

Sartorial,
Ornamental
&
Whimsical

There was an old person of Brigg
Who purchased no end of a wig;
    So that only his nose
    And the ends of his toes
Could be seen when he walked about Brigg.

✳

There was an old man of the Wrekin
Whose shoes made a horrible creaking;
    But they said, 'Tell us whether
    Your shoes are of leather,
Or of what, you old man of the Wrekin?'

✳

'Tis strange how the newspapers honour
A creature that's called prima donna.
    They say not a thing
    Of how she can sing
But reams of the clothes she has on her.

✳

There was an old man of the Cape
Who made himself garments of crêpe;
    When asked, 'Do they tear?'
    He replied, 'Here and there;
But they're perfectly splendid for shape.'

✳

There was a young girl from St Paul
Wore a newspaper dress to a ball;
    But the dress caught on fire
    And burned her entire –
Front page, sporting section and all.

✳

A charming old lady of Settle
For a hat, wore a bright copper kettle.
    When people derided,
    She said, 'I've decided
To show all the neighbours my mettle.'

✳

A thrifty young fellow of Shoreham
Made brown-paper trousers and woreham.
    He looked nice and neat,
    Till he bent in the street
To pick up a coin; then he toreham.

✳

There was a young woman named Frances
Who decided to better her chances
    By cleverly adding
    Appropriate padding
To enlarge all her protuberances.

✳

There was once a lady of Erskine
Who had a remarkably fair skin.
     When I said to her, 'Mabel,
     You look well in sable,'
She replied, 'I look best in my bearskin.'

✳

There was a young dandy of Bute
Who sported a very loud suit.
     When told, 'It's too loud,'
     He archly said, 'How'd
I look in a suit that was mute?'

✳

There was a young lady of Cheltenham
Put on tights just to see how she felt in 'em;
     But she said, with a shout,
     'If you don't pull me out,
I'm sure I shall jolly soon melt in 'em.'

✳

A bald-headed judge named Beauclerk
Fell in love with a maiden seau ferk
     Residing at Bicester,
     Who said, when he kicester,
'I won't wed a man with neau herk!'

✳

There was a young maid in Tahiti
Whom the neighbours considered quite flahiti,
   For if Monday was fine
   She'd hang on the line
An extremely diaphanous nahiti.

✳

   'I wouldn't be bothered with drawers,'
   Says one of our better-known whawers.
      'There isn't a doubt
      I'm better without,
   In handling my everyday chawers.'

✳

   A near-sighted spinster named White
   Wore a suit of pyjamas one night;
      As she happened to pass
      In front of the glass,
   She exclaimed, 'There's a man!' in delight.

✳

The drawers of a spinster from Lavenham
Had rude lim'ricks embroidered in Slav on 'em.
   To her lawyer she said,
   'Burn them all, when I'm dead:
For I'm damned if my nephew is having 'em.'

There was a young thing from Missouri
Who fancied herself as a houri.
   Her friends thus forsook her,
   For a harlot they took her,
And she gave up the role in a fury.

There was a young person of Jaipur
Who fell madly in love with a viper;
  With screams of delight
  He'd retire every night
With the viper concealed in his diaper.

❋

There are some things we mustn't expose
So we hide them away in our clothes.
  Oh, it's shocking to stare
  At what's certainly there –
But why this is so, heaven knows.

❋

There is a sad rumour that Mona
Goes around in a black net kimona.
  Don't think for a minute
  There's anything in it –
Anything much besides Mona.

❋

There was a young woman named Astor
Whose clothes fitted tight as a plaster.
  When she happened to sneeze
  She felt a cold breeze
And knew she had met with disaster.

❋

There was a young lady named Meyer
Whose hemlines got higher and higher;
  But the size of her thighs
  Provoked merely surprise,
And extinguished the flames of desire.

❋

A preacher, who went out to Bali
To change the sartorial folly
   Of the girls, now admits,
    'A good pair of tits
In season can seem rather jolly.'

❋

There was a young man from Australia
Who painted his arse like a dahlia.
   The colour was fine;
    Likewise the design.
But the perfume: ah, that was a failure!

❋

There was a young damsel named Carole
Who liked to play stud for apparel.
   Her opponent's straight flush
   Brought a maidenly blush,
And a hasty trip home in a barrel.

❋

An actor, in furious rage,
Muttered this to an actress on stage,
   'When I'd fallen for you
   I had thought forty-two
Was the size of your breasts – not your age!'

❋

There was a young fellow called Willie
Whose behaviour was frequently silly;
   At a big UN ball,
   Dressed in nothing at all,
He claimed that his costume was Chile.

❋

There was a young lady named Grimes
Who spent all her nickels and dimes
   On satin and lace,
   To hold her in place
And keep her abreast of the times.

Zoological, Oceanographical & Ornithological

There was a young lady of Clare
Who was sadly pursued by a bear;
    When she found she was tired,
    She abruptly expired,
That unfortunate lady of Clare.

✳

There was an old man of the Cape
Who possessed a large Barbary ape,
    Till the ape one dark night
    Set the house all alight,
Which burned that old man of the Cape.

✳

There was an old man who said, 'Hush!
I perceive a young bird in a bush!'
    When they said, 'Is it small?'
    He replied, 'Not at all!
It is four times as big as the bush!'

✳

There was an old man with a beard
Who said, 'It is just as I feared! –
    Two owls and a hen,
    Four larks and a wren,
Have all built their nests in my beard!'

✳

There was an old man of Dundee
Who molested an ape in a tree:
    The result was most horrid,
    All arse and no forehead,
Three balls and a purple goatee.

✳

There was an old man of St Bees
Who was strung in the arm by a wasp.
    When they asked, 'Does it hurt?'
    He replied, 'No, it doesn't!
But I thought all the while 'twas a hornet.'

✳

There once was a plesiosaurus,
Who lived when the world was all porous;
    But it fainted with shame,
    When it first heard its name,
And departed long ages before us.

✳

An amoeba, named Sam, and his brother
Were having a drink with each other;
    In the midst of their quaffing,
    They split themselves laughing,
And each of them now is a mother.

❋

The thoughts of the rabbit on sex
Are seldom, if ever, complex;
   For a rabbit in need
   Is a rabbit indeed,
And does just as a person expects.

❋

An eccentric old person of Slough,
Who took all of his meals with a cow,
   Always said, 'It's uncanny,
   She's so like Aunt Fanny,'
But he never would indicate how.

❋

There was a young charmer named Sheba,
Whose pet was a darling amoeba.
   This queer blob of jelly
   Would lie on her belly
And blissfully murmer, 'Ich liebe.'

❋

There was an old codger of Broome
Who kept a baboon in his room.
   'It reminds me,' he said,
   'Of a friend who is dead.'
But he never would tell us of whom

✳

A lady there was in Antigua
Who said to her spouse, 'What a pigua!'
   He answered, 'My queen,
   Is it my manners you mean,
Or do you refer to my figua?'

✳

Said the crow to a pelican, 'Grant
Me the loan of your bill; for my aunt
   Has asked me to tea.'
   Said the other, 'Not me:
Ask my brother – for this pelican't.'

✳

There was a young man of Westphalia
Who yearly got tail-ier and tail-ier,
   Till he took on the shape
   Of a Barbary ape
With the consequent paraphernalia.

✳

An adventurous fun-loving polyp
Propositioned a cute little scallop
   Down under the sea;
   'Nothing doing,' said she;
'By Triton – you think I'm a trollop?'

❋

Said an eminent, erudite ermine:
'There's one thing I cannot determine:
   When a dame wears my coat
   She's a person of note;
When I wear it, I'm called only vermin.'

❋

There was an old lady of Wales
Who lived upon mussels and snails.
   On growing a shell,
   She exclaimed, 'Just as well! –
It will save me in bonnets and veils.'

✳

A hen who resided in Reading
Attended a gentleman's wedding.
   As she walked up the aisle
   The guests had to smile
In spite of the tears they were shedding.

✳

You will find by the banks of the Nile
The haunts of the great crocodile.
   He will welcome you in
   With an innocent grin
Which gives way to a satisfied smile.

✳

At the zoo I remarked to an emu,
'I cannot pretend I esteem you;
   You're a greedy old bird
   And your walk is absurd;
And not even your feathers redeem you!'

✳

There was a young woman named Sue
Who saw a strange beast in the zoo;
   When she asked, 'Is it old?'
   She firmly was told,
'No! Certainly not! It is gnu.'

✳

A disgusting young man named McGill
Made his neighbours exceedingly ill
   When they learned of his habits
   Involving white rabbits
And a bird with a flexible bill.

✳

A wonderful bird is the pelican
His bill can hold more than his belican.
   He can take in his beak
   Enough food for a week.
But nobody knows how the helican.

✳

A creature of charm is the gerbil
Its diet's exclusively herbal;
   It browses all day
   On great bunches of hay,
And farts with an elegant burble.

✳

There was a young man named Colquhoun
Who kept as a pet a babuhoun.
   His mother said, 'Cholmondeley,
   I don't think it's quite colmondeley
To feed your babuhoun with a spuhoun '

✳

A flea and a fly in a flue
Were imprisoned, so what could they do?
  Said the fly: 'Let us flee!'
  Said the flea: 'Let us fly!'
So they flew through a flaw in the flue.

✳

As he filled up his order book's pp.,
He declared, 'I demand higher ww.!'
  So he struck for more pay
  But, alas, they now say
He is sweeping out elephants' cc.

✳

A stately giraffe, when he necks,
Or a hippo, when he's having sex,
  Aren't worth a tut-tut
  To the bellowing rut
Of the great Tyrannosaurus Rex.

✳

There once was a gnu in a zoo
Who tired of the same daily view.
  To seek a new sight,
  He stole out one night,
And where he went, gnobody gnew.

✳

An old maid in the land of Aloha
Got wrapped in the coils of a boa,
   And as the snake squeezed,
   The old maid, not displeased,
Cried, 'Darling! I love it! Samoa.'

✳

There was an old spinster from Fife
Who had never been kissed in her life;
   Along came a cat
   And she said, 'I'll kiss that,'
But the cat meowed, 'Not on your life!'

❋

The eminent Mme DeVue
Was born in a cage at the zoo,
   And the curious rape
   Which made her an ape
Is highly fantastic, if true.

❋

A broken-clown harlot named Tupps
Was heard to confess in her cups:
   'The height of my folly
   Was diddling a collie –
But I got a nice price for the pups.'

❋

A herder who hailed from Terre Haute
Fell in love with a young nanny-goat.
   The daughter he sired
   Was greatly admired
For her beautiful angora coat.

❋

There was a young man of Wood's Hole
Who had an affair with a mole.
   Though a bit of a nancy
   He did like to fancy
Himself in a dominant role.

✻

There was a young fellow named Price
Who dabbled in all sorts of vice:
    He had virgins and boys
    And mechanical toys
And on Mondays he meddled with mice.

✻

A professor of ethical culture
Once said to his class: ' 'Twould insult your
    Intelligence if
    I said I got stiff
For anything less than a vulture.'

✻

A fellow who fucked as but few can
Had a fancy to try with a toucan.
    He owned like a man
    The collapse of his plan:
'I can't – but I bet none of you can!'

✻

There was a young woman called Myrtle
Who once was seduced by a turtle;
    The result of this mate
    Was five crabs and a skate,
Thus proving the turtle was fertile.

✳

Said a lynx as he playfully threw
His mate down a well in Peru,
   'Relax, dearest Thora,
    Please don't be angora,
I was only artesian you.'

✳

A southern hillbilly named Hollis
Used possums and snakes as his solace;
   His children had scales
    And prehensile tails
And voted for Governor Wallace.

✳

A round-bottomed babe from Mobile
Longed for years to be screwed by a seal,
   But out at the zoo,
    They just said: 'No can do' –
Though the seal is all hot for the deal.

✳

Said a guardsman, observing his charger:
'I do wish my tassel were larger.
   Could I change with my horse,
    I should do so, of course,
And put in for high stud fees – like Rajah!'

✻

A scandal involving an oyster
Sent the Countess of Clewes to a cloister.
   She preferred it in bed
   To the Count, so she said,
Being longer and stronger and moister.

✻

There was a young girl of Batonger
Used to bring herself off with a conger.
   When asked how it feels
   To be pleasured by eels,
She said, 'Just like a man, only longer.'

✳

I was thrilled when I went to the zoo:
They allowed me to bugger the gnu!
    An FRZS
    Remarked to me, 'Yes,
It's a privilege granted to few.'

✳

There was an old man of the Cape
Who buggered a Barbary ape.
    The ape said, 'You fool!
    You've got a square tool;
You've buggered my arse out of shape.'

✳

There was a young man of Bengal
Who went to a fancy-dress ball.
    Just for a whim
    He dressed up as a quim,
And was had by the dog in the hall.

✳

There was a musician named Royce
Who, tired both of women and boys,
    Remarked with a sigh,
    'I fear I must try
Alsatians for my sexual joys.'

✳

There was a young fellow named Spiegel
Who had an affair with a seagull.
    What's worse (do you see?),
    It wasn't a she
But a he-gull and that is illegal.

✳

There was a young man of St Paul
Whose prick was exceedingly small.
    He could bugger a bug
    At the edge of a rug,
And the bug hardly felt it at all.

✳

There was an old man of Santander
Who attempted to bugger a gander.
    But that virtuous bird
    Plugged its ass with a turd,
And refused to such low tastes to pander.

✳

There was a young man in Peru
Who had nothing whatever to do,
    So he flew to the garret
    And buggered the parrot,
And sent the result to the zoo.

✳

A German explorer named Schlichter
Had a yen for a boa constrictor;
    When he lifted the tail,
    Achtung! 'Twas a male –
The constrictor, not Schlichter, was victor.

✳

There was a young girl who would make
Advances to snake after snake.
    She said, 'I'm not vicious,
    But so superstitious!
I do it for grandmother's sake.'

✳

There once was a young man named Cyril
Who was had in a wood by a squirrel,
    And he liked it so good
    That he stayed in the wood
Just as long as the squirrel stayed virile.

✳

An Argentine gaucho named Bruno
Once said, 'There is one thing I do know:
    A woman is fine
    And a sheep is divine,
But a llama is *numero uno*!'

✳

There was a young lady of Rhodes
Who sinned in unusual modes.
    At the height of her fame
    She abruptly became
The mother of four dozen toads.

✳

You've heard of the Duchess of York?
She's twice been blessed by the stork.
    The Duke he will fuck
    Naught else but a duck,
While the Duchess she frequents the park.

✳

A very polite man named Hawarden
Went out to plant flowers in his gawarden.
    If h e trod on a slug,
    A worm or a bug,
He would instantly say, 'I beg pawarden.'

✳

There was an old Scot named MacTavish
Who attempted a gibbon to ravish,
    But the object o f rape
    Was the wrong sex of ape –
And the anthropoid ravished MacTavish.

❋

There was a young man from New Haven
Who had an affair with a raven.
   He said with a grin,
   As he wiped of his chin,
'Nevermore! Nevermore!'

❋

As dull as the life of the cloister
(Except it's a little bit moister),
   Mutatis mutandum
   Non est disputandum,
There's no thrill in sex for the oyster.

❋

A gloomy old man of Khartoum
Kept two playful old sheep in his room
   'They remind me,' he said,
   Of two friends who are dead.
But he never would tell us of whom.

❋

There was an old dame of Malacca
Who smoked such atrocious tobacca
   That when tigers came near
   They trembled with fear,
And didn't attempt to attack her.

✳

There once was a Duchess of Belvoir
Who slept with her golden retrelvoir.
   Said the choleric Duke:
   'The old girl makes me puke
And but for the dog I would lelvoir.'

✳

There was a young lady of Riga
Who smiled as she rode on a tiger;
   They returned from the ride
   With the lady inside
And the smile on the face of the tiger.

✳

An extremely short-kilted North Briton
Sat carelessly down on a kitten;
   But the kitten had claws –
   The immediate cause
Of the Scotsman's abrupt circumcision.

✳

Consider the poor hippopotamus:
His life is unduly monotonous.
   He lives half asleep
   At the edge of the deep
And his face is as big as his bottom is.

✳

You'd require an extremely long scarf
If you happened to be a giraffe;
   They get very hoarse
   In the winter, of course,
And a sore throat is no cause to laugh.

✳

A barber who lived in Belgravia,
Well known for his faultless behaviour,
   Remarked to a baboon
   Who came in his saloon,
'Do sit down – but I'm damned if I'll
                  shave yer.'

✳

A cheerful old bear at the zoo
Could always find something to do.
   When it bored him to go
   On a walk to and fro
He reversed it and walked fro and to.

✳

If you meet with the Indian rhinoceros,
You might think he just looks preposterous.
   But how would you like
   A nose with a spike?
It would make even Gandhi ferocerous.

✳

If there's one thing that nature has taught us
It's the virtues of being a tortoise.
   They can slumber, I hear,
   More than half of the year
In the depths of their snug winter-quartoise.

✳

   The elephant never forgets:
Neither messages, shopping or debts.
   He can take in his trunk
   A whole load of junk –
And the small ones make fabulous pets!

337

✳

A cat in despondency sighed
And resolved to commit suicide.
    She passed under the wheels
    Of eight automobiles,
And after the ninth one she died.

✳

There was a young girl called O'Brien
Who tried to teach hymns to a lion.
    Of the lady, there's some
    In the lion's tum-tum:
The rest twangs a harp up in Zion.

✳

According to experts, the oyster
In its shell (or crustacean cloister)
    May at any time be
    Either he or a she –
Or both, if it should be its choister.

✳

A tiger, by taste anthropophagous,
Felt a yearning within his oesophagus;
    He spied a fat Brahmin
    And growled, 'What's the harm in
A peripatetic sarcophagus?'

✳

The wife of a farmer in Stoke,
Always one for a dubious joke,
    Caught his sow in the act
    And reported the fact
To her spouse as 'a pig in a poke'.

✳

It is the unfortunate habit
Of the rabbit to breed like a rabbit.
    One can say without question
    This leads to congestion
In the burrows that rabbits inhabit.

✳

There once was a lady of Dover
Who said to her husband, 'Move over!
    I don't give a damn
    For the charms of a man –
Now come along, Rover!'

✳

There was an old man of Tashkent
Who slept with twelve goats in a tent.
    When asked: 'Do they smell?'
    He said: 'Oh, yes, quite well . . .
But so far they don't mind my scent.'

. . . and One for the Road

*

There was a young lady from Gloucester
Whose parents they thought they had lost her –
　　For there on the grass
　　Were the marks of her arse
And the knees of the man who had crossed her.

Index

✳

341

INDEX

INDEX

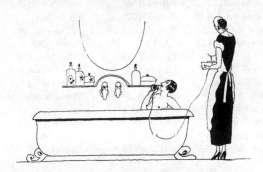